<u>Acknowledgments</u>

Thank you to my editor, Bobbi Sheahan, for your keen insight, encouragement, and guidance during the editing of this book.

To my husband, Scott, thank you for your unwavering love and continued support in all that I do. And to my son, Thomas, thank you for showing me how to parent you. You are a wonderful teacher.

PLAN B

Empowering the Single Parent, to Benefit Their Child with Autism

Karra Barber-Wada

Plan B: Empowering the Single Parent, to Benefit Their Child with Autism

All marketing and publishing rights guaranteed to and reserved by:

FUTURE HORIZONSINC.

721 W. Abram Street
Arlington, Texas 76013
800·489·0727
817·277·0727
817·277·2270 (fax)
E-mail: *info@fhautism.com*
www.fhautism.com

ISBN: 978-1-935274-79-7

This book is dedicated to my son, Thomas, and to every single parent who is raising a child with special needs. You are one of the noble, courageous, and dedicated—truly an unsung hero of our time.

Table of Contents _____

Introduction _____

A large percentage of the parents raising children with an autism spectrum disorder (ASD) in the U.S. are doing so alone. The fact is, divorce happens, circumstances change, and life goes on. The ability to create a "Plan B" and put it into action is demonstrated over and over again in this book.

Over the years, I have met and admired many single parents of children with ASD. I've respected the love and commitment they've shown to their children and marveled at how they too have "survived" the day-to-day challenges of parenting alone. By offering a snippet of my own personal story, along with a compilation of other single-parenting accounts of separation and divorce, I hope to encourage you to recognize that you too can incorporate a new plan of action if you find yourself in a similar situation.

This book is filled with steps you can implement to establish a new "Plan B" for yourself and your child or children. I've broken these steps down into three categories, which will be accompanied by the following helpful graphics throughout the book:

♡ Emotional steps: Promoting feelings of well-being for you and your child

☾ Practical steps: Thinking, planning, brainstorming

✋ Actual steps: Implementing your plan of action

I've also included a wealth of parenting tips to use when you're faced with taking care of a child with ASD as a single parent. So—let's discover what developing a "Plan B" is all about.

Today

When I arrived home tonight, I discovered my son slumped over, asleep at his desk. His glasses rested crookedly on his face. Nearby, I found his laptop open and still humming. *Good grief,* I thought. I glanced at the clock over his bed. It was 1 AM! *How long had he been studying?* I wondered. As I scanned his room, I noticed a bunch of balled-up pieces of paper in the trash can by his desk. I picked one up and flattened it out against the desktop. On it was a half-written essay about the comparison between good and evil. His SAT practice book was cracked open to a page on which he had highlighted test questions. What is an auxiliary? What is the perfect participle? What is a hypothesis? There was a collection of vocabulary flash cards scattered across his desk. He must have been reviewing the materials one last time before taking his SAT exam in the morning. *He's come a long way,* I told myself.

And so have I.

My son Thomas has Asperger's syndrome. As a toddler, he had limited language skills, obvious processing difficulties, and complex social challenges. Today, you would never know that Thomas understands the concept of a "Plan B" and uses it as a coping mechanism. At age 17, Thomas is a senior at a college preparatory high school. He is awaiting his SAT results and is looking forward to touring colleges and planning for his future. I'm proud of his personal achievements, just as I'm proud to have prepared both him and myself for the unanticipated situations that arise in life.

Having been a single parent for the past 13 years, I've been able to observe Thomas's progress and reflect on my journey with him and the steps we've taken together. Most were wonderful, some were painful, but all have been survivable. Raising Thomas as a single parent has been one of the most difficult and rewarding experiences in my life. Despite the numerous challenges we've endured over the years, I am thankful to have learned a lot about myself. Most profoundly, I have learned about my resilience as an individual, my commitment as a parent, and my determination as a child advocate. Raising a child on the autism spectrum by myself has provided me with the opportunity to recognize when and how to implement a "Plan B."

When circumstances change unexpectedly in everyday life, having the ability to develop and/or accept a different plan of action (a "Plan B") is essential. Thomas and I know this firsthand.

In this book, I will share a few details with you about my life with Thomas, to give you a frame of reference and to illustrate the progress I've made as a single parent of a child with Asperger's. However, my true goal is to share relevant information with you. I hope to inspire you, so that you too can devise your own "Plan B" if you've determined that your "Plan A" isn't working out as you'd planned.

CHAPTER 18:
Single-Parenting a Child with Asperger's Syndrome

Our Story

Shortly after Thomas's 4th birthday, I finally acknowledged that although my husband and I had been living together as a married couple, we'd been living our lives separately and were extremely disconnected from each other. Despite the fact that we were both devoted and loving parents to our son, after many months of deep contemplation, we eventually came to the conclusion that we'd be better parents if we were no longer a couple. Ultimately, we agreed to put our emotional selves aside for a time and make Thomas our number-one priority. In doing so, we made every attempt to make joint decisions regarding Thomas, which at times was very difficult. We made great efforts to balance his basic needs and his special needs to the best of our ability.

One thing was abundantly clear: We both loved our son dearly, and that would never change, despite the shift in our personal relationship. Our divorce was finalized when Thomas was 5. Although this was a very difficult decision, I knew I had to create a "Plan B" for myself and for Thomas. In my new role as a single parent, I needed to shape a different course for us as we moved forward.

"Plan B" in Motion

As with so many single parents who find themselves at this kind of a crossroads, at times I felt completely overwhelmed in my new and seemingly solo role. Nevertheless, I knew that what I did and how I chose to view my new situation would profoundly affect my future, as well as Thomas'. This was a time in my life when I had to look deep inside and hold on to the strong, solid, and capable person I knew myself to be. I kept reminding myself that I was resourceful and resilient. I was certainly someone who had the endurance and the wisdom to start over and support Thomas and his special needs (my new mantra). And, as tough as it was at first—and it was tough—I deliberately chose to regard my circumstances as unrealized opportunities for our future. That belief, along with a healthy dose of determination, were the motivators I needed to start again with a new plan of action—what I called our "Plan B."

Steps Forward

As I began taking steps toward rebuilding my life as a single parent, I knew I needed to concentrate on my *emotional* (feeling), *practical* (thinking/planning), and *actual* (doing) states of being. So, that's what I did.

○ The *emotional* steps I took were deliberately intended to keep myself and Thomas emotionally steady during a time when we needed the most reassurance.

☀ *Practically* speaking, the mental steps I took included *(a)* realizing my options, *(b)* embracing the new responsibilities that come with being a single parent of a special-needs child, and *(c)* developing a plan of action.

 The *actual* steps I took involved *(a)* focusing primarily on Thomas, his special needs, and the structure he required to maintain his continued growth and development and *(b)* executing my plan of action.

To gain support, I quickly joined an autism spectrum disorder (ASD) parent support group with other parents who could relate to my circumstances. Eventually, I started my own monthly support group for parents, both single and coupled, with children on the autism spectrum; this is something you can do, too. Collectively, the group provided a platform to share relevant information, community resources, and personal experiences (both positive and negative) for others to learn from. Ultimately, these group meetings helped to produce "road maps" for parents whose children had received new diagnoses and for families who were entering into uncharted territory in their lives.

Emotional Steps Are Important _____

Don't suffer in silence. Although many parents may consider themselves strong and able to carry the weight of the world on their shoulders, the magnitude of raising a child with autism by oneself can be an utterly paralyzing experience at times. Divorce is a life-altering decision that affects everyone differently, on many emotional levels.

Reaching Out for Support: Joanne's Story

"I can't handle this … I just can't do it anymore." This became Joanne's ongoing internal dialogue.

With an uninvolved ex and her family in a different state, Joanne struggled with juggling her work as a part-time nurse and raising her twin toddlers, one of whom was autistic. After 9 months of going it alone, with dirty laundry mounting, dishes piled in the sink, and two tired and screaming toddlers underfoot, one evening Joanne fell apart. "What am I doing? I cannot go on like this," Joanne sobbed to a girlfriend on the phone. "I don't know what I was thinking. I thought that with my ex out of the picture, it would be easier. I'm a capable, educated woman, and I convinced myself that I could hold down a job, care for my kids, and manage as a single parent, all without asking for help from anyone. But I feel like I'm drowning. What in the world is wrong with me?" Joanne was at her wits' end.

Finally, Joanne asked her friends for help. A group of Joanne's girlfriends (who were mothers themselves) got together, stepped in, and took charge. They created a schedule in which they offered their time to Joanne and her twins—something Joanne needed desperately. One friend committed to care for Joanne's twins one afternoon a week, so she could take care of basic household tasks, such as grocery shopping, banking, and doing laundry. Another friend agreed to carpool the twins to and from preschool twice weekly, while a third friend invited Joanne to come to a weekly yoga class for some adult quiet time.

Because Joanne's ex had chosen not to have an active role in his children's lives after their split, Joanne said she felt guilty and was overcompensating for her ex's absence at the expense of her own mental, emotional, and physical health. When she finally did ask for help, she was able to lessen her load and refocus her energies on herself and her children—her ultimate goal!

"It's silly when I think about it now … I was just too proud to ask for help in the beginning. I'm glad I eventually realized the value of letting go of the façade of having to be the perfect mother," Joanne admitted. "News flash: Perfection is overrated!"

○ Take Emotional Steps Forward _____

Ask for Emotional Assistance

If you have a child with ASD, your decision to divorce or parent solo becomes substantially more complex. If you are considering separation or divorce, perhaps seeking out couples' counseling, family counseling, or individual therapy from a licensed professional would be useful during and/or after that process. Parents can struggle during this transitional time, often as much as their children. We need to ask for assistance when we require it. Family, friends, neighbors, church members, and coworkers can be good supporters. Take comfort in knowing that you are doing the very best you can in any given moment.

TIP Designate one afternoon a week as "grandparent time" or "family-friend time." Use these afternoons to rejuvenate yourself, while your children enjoy someone else's undivided attention.

Give Yourself Time to Heal after Ending a Relationship

When a relationship or marriage ends, it's common to feel guilty, devastated, anxious, depressed, sad, angry, or even relieved. Allow yourself to feel any or all of these emotions and more. You've just been through a life-altering change. Healing happens over a period of time, not overnight. Allow yourself the time you need to process this enormous decision that affects both you and your child. Ending any kind of relationship can be a major loss, and you will need a period of time to grieve and/or cope with the feelings and emotions that come up.

TIP Take breaks regularly. Make them part of your routine. Read a book, take a nap, see a movie, attend a yoga class, take a walk, or engage in other calming activities, like mediation or massage. It's okay to take some time for yourself to reflect on your past and find solace. It's a process. Give yourself permission to take care of your own needs. Parents are people, too!

Surround Yourself with Those Who Understand Your Situation

Accept the transformation in your life and embrace the new possibilities for personal growth. Your circumstances are changing, and your responsibilities are shifting, as well. Find the confidence within yourself to trust in your ability as a parent. Surround yourself with family and friends who love you and understand your choices. Spend time with those who believe in you as a person and respect your decisions as a parent. Life can be hard sometimes. Acknowledge it and try and move forward. An optimistic outlook goes a long way. Find a support group of like-minded people who can provide you with wisdom and encouragement, as well as assistance.

Feeling lonely and overwhelmed from the events of the day is common. Accept help and understanding from those who accept you and your situation.

> **TIP** Contact a friend, relative, or counselor or someone who will lend you support and encouragement on a regular basis. Try to focus on one positive thought each day before you go to sleep and/or when you wake up in the morning. Concentrate on what you are thankful for. Ask yourself, what did your child do today that made you smile? What made you especially happy? What made you laugh out loud?

Connect with Other Parents Who Have Children with Special Needs

Single-parenting a child with ASD can feel isolating and terribly overwhelming at times—particularly in the beginning. Recognize that you are not alone and that there are supports out there for you. Consider seeking out other single parents with special-needs children who have been through something similar and can share their experiences with you. Find support, strategies, and even solutions from those who have walked your path and can help you find your way. If it's helpful to you, share your circumstances with other parents. Join a support group in a community with seasoned parents who can provide ideas and alternatives when it comes to resources and services for you and your child.

TIP If possible, join a local or online ASD parent support group. Many support groups are listed online, if you search for "local autism parent groups." If there isn't a local ASD parent group in your area, start one. Public places such as libraries, bookstores, and coffee shops are usually centrally located and make great locations to hold parent meetings. Typically the venue is free, and parking is accessible. You can advertise your new group to other parents of children with ASD by posting a free ad in your local newspaper, on online ASD blogs, or in online newsletters. Local disability agencies can also help you spread the word.

Move Forward Toward a New Future

A positive attitude will help you build confidence. Focus on yourself and your new life as a single parent. Realize that the past is the past, and the present is now. Moving forward toward a new beginning can be extremely intimidating, a welcome relief, or a combination of both. Either way, remember that although you are only one person, you are a capable person. Don't be afraid to establish practical goals for yourself and your life, even if they seem out of reach initially. Revel in your newfound independence. This is your time to start fresh. Recreate yourself.

Dust off your employment skills and/or brush up on new ones. If you plan on returning to the workforce, take a class at the community college in a field of interest to you. Spruce up your résumé with skills you've acquired as a stay-at-home parent (examples might be PTA member, committee organizer, troop fundraiser, or board participant). If you have a college degree but you need recent work experience in a specific area, volunteer your skills. If you plan to be a nurse, volunteer at a hospital. If you want to be a teacher, volunteer at a school.

If your goal is to work with animals, intern at an animal shelter. Direct your time and energies into a career path you wish to pursue. To get the word out, start networking with friends. Tell them you are actively looking for work experience and ask them for formal or informal introductions to people who can help you. Make a point to attend your friends' parties, your child's school functions, and your neighbors' summer barbecues. Be sure to mingle with new people and establish connections with acquaintances. You never know who can help you achieve your goals in life.

Networking Works: Suzie's Story

Suzie and her 12-year-old son Jack wanted to remain in the family home (and in a familiar neighborhood) after Suzie and her ex split up. To do that, Suzie knew she needed to get a job that would enable her to afford the mortgage payment. It was the end of the summer. Jack was ready to return to school, while Suzie was preparing to re-enter the work force. Because she'd been a stay-at-home mom since Jack received a diagnosis of autism at the age of 3, Suzie realized it could be difficult for her to find a job without any recent employment experience. Although she had worked as a freelance writer years ago, since the time of Jack's diagnosis, she hadn't picked up a pen, let alone written anything worthy of submission to a publisher. Instead, her days were spent advocating for Jack. She realized that for more than a decade, her whole life had revolved around Jack and his special needs.

Feeling out of touch with the professional world, Suzie decided to meet with several of the gal pals from her book club, and she started networking. She was determined to keep her house! Over coffee, Suzie and her gal pals (who worked in various fields) brainstormed possible employment options that would match Suzie's skill set. What were Suzie's abilities and experiences? Together, they quickly listed Suzie's strengths and talents and tallied up her recent "non-employment" accomplishments: She was the PTA president, a special-education parent liaison, an autism advocate extraordinaire, not to mention assistant to the swim coach, scout troop leader, theater club mom, and participant in any other community activity Jack attended. In a "light bulb moment," one of Suzie's pals offered to introduce Suzie to her boss, who was the editor of the local newspaper.

With Suzie's prior freelance experience and her obvious knowledge about and regular involvement in community-centered activities, Suzie wound up getting a job with the local newspaper to cover their weekly community events. Mission accomplished—through networking!

TIP Are you starting over in the workforce and wondering where to begin? Start by making a list of your interests, experiences, strengths, talents, and accomplishments. Build your résumé with all of the information compiled from your lists. Next, make a "networking" list of people whom you believe to be helpful in facilitating the achievement of your goal. The hope is that you will find employment in a position where your interests, experience, and skill set are a good match with the job requirements.

EXERCISE 1: *Returning to the Workforce*

Complete the following exercise to help you identify what sort of skills and interests you bring to the table and whom you might connect with to find employment that's a good fit for you.

1. **INTERESTS:** What do you like to do?

_____

_____

_____

2. **EXPERIENCE:** What work or volunteer experience do you have?

_____

_____

_____

3. **STRENGTHS:** What are your abilities?

_____

_____

_____

4. **TALENTS:** What are you good at?

_____

_____

_____

5. **ACCOMPLISHMENTS:** What have you attained, achieved, or mastered?

_____

_____

_____

6. **RÉSUMÉ-BUILDING:** Build your résumé by using the information you listed above.

7. **NETWORKING:** Make a list of your friends, acquaintances, relatives, and neighbors. Who might be able to help you?

_____

_____

_____

○ What Are Your Emotional Steps Forward?

Write down five "emotional steps forward" that you feel will help keep you and your child(ren) emotionally steady during a time when you need the most reassurance.

1. _____

2. _____

3. _____

4. _____

5. _____

🜚 Practical Steps_____

For families who have a child on the autism spectrum, divorce can become exceedingly challenging. Children's emotional states are altered, their treatment programs are affected, and their everyday routines become more unpredictable.

Moving Forward: Erica's Story

Six-year-old Erica received a diagnosis of pervasive developmental disorder at age 3. After a long and laborious court battle, her parents' divorce became final, and primary custody of Erica and her younger sister Amanda was awarded to their mother, Lisa. Their father's (Jon's) visitation schedule consisted of alternating weekends, holidays, and summer vacations. This transition was especially difficult for Erica, as demonstrated by her constant meltdowns, bed-wetting, and irregular sleep patterns. To complicate matters, Lisa took a part-time job as a paralegal and moved the girls 50 miles away from where Jon resided when Erica was in first grade. This created logistical challenges for Jon, in terms of visitation and attending school-related activities.

"This was a very hard time for all of us," said Lisa. "Jon and I were not on good terms when we filed for divorce. Erica was having outbursts at school. She wasn't sleeping or eating well, either. In the midst of all of this, I got a job and moved out of town. Jon's work record had been spotty, and our finances had been limited. Although it was in the middle of the school year, I had to make the decision to relocate for financial reasons. I knew I wanted to register Erica in a special-education program right away, so she could get back on track in a new school as soon as possible. I was aware that the combination of all of those changes would most likely complicate things for Jon and the girls, particularly Erica, but I felt I had no choice. We needed a steady income, and I could provide that better than Jon at that point."

As Lisa was getting situated at her new job and settling into her new apartment in a new city with the girls, she prepared to meet with the officials at Erica's new school to create an Individualized Education Program (IEP) for Erica. Gathering old medical records and neuropsychology reports for Erica's IEP meeting was a full-time job. Erica had so many documents to organize. Having gone through the IEP process before at Erica's previous school, Lisa and Jon were aware of the procedures necessary to reinstate Erica's IEP. Although Erica had previously come from a special-needs classroom environment, her progress had been clearly noted in many academic and psychological evaluations.

The IEP team at Erica's new school took their time in reviewing her assessments and all other pertinent information. Eventually, the IEP team agreed to Erica's new placement in a general-education classroom, with part-time assistance from an educational aide. The new IEP team also agreed to provide Erica with other special-education services, which included an hour of individualized speech and occupational therapy per week. Even attending a weekly social-skills "lunch bunch" group with her typically developing peers was written into Erica's new IEP.

"Jon and I were pleasantly surprised—ecstatic actually— with the support services provided by the new school district. Also, Jon's health insurance plan continued to provide Erica with an additional hour a week of speech therapy from a private practitioner. I must confess, although Erica's school program was a good one, the adjustment to all the new changes affected her behavior at school and at home for some time," Lisa added.

Finances were an ongoing issue for Lisa and Jon. Jon's monthly child support payments were nominal. As the primary custodian for both children, Lisa still struggled to make ends meet by working part time. This meant she had to adhere to a strict household budget to be able to live within her means.

"Fortunately, my income level as a single parent made me eligible to receive a cost reduction for after-school child care through the local YMCA. This was something I desperately needed as a working single mom," said Lisa.

☀ Take Practical Steps Forward_____

Obtain Legal Advice, Counsel, and/or Mediation Intervention

Often, you will find that as you become a single parent, you may require legal advice, expertise, and/or other outside assistance to facilitate the dissolution of your marriage. Do your homework and gather any pertinent information you need for yourself and your child regarding your specific situation. Research and understand your legal rights, options, and obligations.

When it comes to having custody of a special-needs child, certain provisions may need to be considered for the division of child custody and financial obligations as they relate to child support, overall settlement, and possible future guardianship of your child (depending on the state you live in). In most states, child support ends after the child turns 18 or finishes college, but every state has different laws and procedures. When you have a special-needs child, often a financial assistance plan can be developed and agreed upon between both parties (for example, this can be spelled out in a living trust).

TIP If you are hiring an attorney to handle your divorce, ask for references. An attorney with experience in representing parents with special-needs children is preferable. Each state has different laws about marriage, divorce, spousal support, and child custody and/or parenting time. Make and keep copies of all records and relevant documents regarding your dissolution of marriage in case a document is lost or misfiled at a court clerk's office.

Preparing to Transition to a Single-Family Residence

Making the decision to physically change your place of residence is difficult on many levels. Logistically, having to organize and actually move your belongings from one location to another can be stressful for anyone, particularly for a child on the autism spectrum. Most likely, your ex will maintain shared custody of your child (also called *parenting time* in some states). With that in mind, many children with ASD may require special consideration when it comes moving their belongings. If and how your child's belongings will be moved from one location to another may be a big decision that affects your child with ASD greatly. Because this issue can be an extremely sensitive topic for your youngster, determining how the process will be handled should be coordinated by both parents prior to the move.

TIP ▶ When appropriate, sit down with your child and decide together which of her things will be located at which family home. Having your child participate in the decision-making may help alleviate any concerns she may have, while giving her a sense of control. Your child may decide to keep a few personal items with her to transport back and forth between homes. The idea is to allow her to engage in the decision-making process. Don't be surprised if you have to repeatedly dispel concerns about your child's possessions. Anxiety is so often part of everyday life for those with autism. You can help alleviate that anxiety by providing your child with detailed information and reassurance about upcoming events or changes. This is useful for all children, at any age.

Set Up Financial and Budgetary Goals

Finances are typically a top concern when dealing with a special-needs child, owing to having to maintain the services required to accommodate her developmental needs. Optimally, both parents will agree to financially provide for their child's special services. If needed, the legal system can help determine the division of financial responsibilities regarding a child. As a single parent, it's best to establish new budgetary goals for yourself and your child on the basis of your income and expenses and the limitations of a single income. Prioritize your basic living expenses and create a new budget on the basis of what's absolutely essential. Remember, concerns involving finances are big for parents in general. But for single parents who are raising special-needs children, these concerns are magnified and must be dealt with in an organized and systematic manner to be effective.

For example, when I first became a single parent and was living on virtually one income, I had to recalculate my budget to fit my new circumstances in a way that allowed me to reprioritize my goals for myself and my son. I made a list of nonnegotiable items and compared it with things I'd like to continue to have and financially manage. This made it easy for me to see exactly what I was dealing with, how my priorities had to temporarily change, and thus how my choices would affect my finances. Over time, as I made more money, I reevaluated my priorities and added in more of the things I was able to afford prior to my divorce. It was a choice—and it was empowering to know that *I was in charge of my choices.*

TIP Balancing finances can be a tricky thing. If you find that finances are limited because of the shift in your marital or relationship situation and you can no longer provide for your child's special-needs services in the same way you did before, make a list of services and prioritize them according to your child's greatest need at the moment. For example, if your child's speech is delayed, but she is making definite improvement, consider keeping her speech therapy but reducing the frequency (I did this for my own son). The same goes for occupational therapy, psychotherapy, behavioral therapy, and the like. Remember, no decision is set in stone. When your financial situation improves, reevaluate your child's needs and decide if extended, altered, or additional services are necessary.

Create a Balance between Children, Work, and Home Life

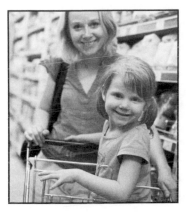

As a newly single parent, sustaining a healthy balance between your life at work and your life at home with your special-needs child can be hard. Time-management skills and organizational strategies can help you prioritize the division of these fundamental components. As you prioritize your time and plans, however, recognize that things may not always go as planned. Realize that schedules may change unexpectedly. Teach your child with autism to be flexible with those changes and to be open to a "Plan B." You may even make up scenarios with your child, creating an "A Plan" and a "B Plan" for certain situations. Have your child practice being "flexible" with unexpected outcomes. Be clear with your children about expectations and responsibilities—yours and theirs.

TIP Try and share at least one family meal together every day. Include your child in household tasks and family activities, such as grocery shopping or making a family meal. Create new memories and share new experiences with your child. Help your child understand that she is an integral part of your "new" family unit. Sit down with your child and create a plan or schedule for the day or week. Let her know that her input is important to you.

Develop a Family System to Co-Parent with Your Ex (Whenever Possible)

Establish an effective and appropriate method of communicating with your ex, where you express yourself openly and directly but never through your child. If appropriate, designate a specific day or time of the week when the two of you can meet and discuss issues regarding your child. Try not to speak negatively of the other parent in front of your child. To demonstrate "co-parenting," when disciplining your child, try and establish consistency by respecting rules and consequences in both homes (whenever possible). For example, if your child loses computer privileges in one home, try and be consistent with the same consequence in both homes. This may or may not be possible all of the time (or any of the time). But, it's important for your special-needs child to understand that each parent may approach things differently, rather than one parent being "right" and the other parent being "wrong." I can't express this point strongly enough: Even if you don't agree with the consequence given to your child by the other parent, working together shows your child that both parents are united in their parenting. For example, when my ex imposed a consequence on my son after he pushed another child at recess, I carried out the consequence in my home, as well.

NOTE: Oftentimes, local community colleges or community centers offer parenting classes that address co-parenting topics after a divorce.

TIP Whenever possible, maintain a cordial relationship with your ex. Try to exchange information about your child regularly in person, over the telephone, or through e-mail.

If issues arise that require your joint attention (examples would be dietary issues, medical problems, bullying at school, behavioral outbursts, psychological concerns, and the like), offer to meet with the other parent. In fact, whenever you can, try and meet with the other parent regularly to share positive information about your child (and even with your child, when appropriate). This provides an opportunity to have positive discussions about your child (examples might include making progress with peers in social settings, reaching academic achievements, attaining behavioral benchmarks, and so on).

I realize that oftentimes, especially at first, co-parenting with a disengaged or uncooperative parent can be challenging. This becomes even more complicated when you are co-parenting a child with autism. However, how you deal with this kind of situation will directly affect the potential outcome. When effective communication about your child is not possible between you and your ex, try to exchange information by using nonconfrontational methods (perhaps via attorneys and/or in writing). In fact, there may be no other way around it. E-mail can be very useful in this regard. Although this may not be optimal, it may be necessary in the beginning.

Hopefully, over time, the communication between you and your ex will improve to the point where you can have direct contact. Believe it or not, many contentious relationships improve or "normalize" after a while. I have known several couples that weren't on speaking terms during their divorce but were able to finally co-parent their special-needs child effectively because they put the best interest of their child first. If you need assistance when it comes to how to communicate effectively with your ex, perhaps you can seek counseling or therapy (perhaps involving role-playing) so you can generate ideas about how best to cope with a difficult ex.

What Are Your Practical Steps Forward?

Write down the practical steps forward that will assist you in exploring options, taking action, and embracing new responsibilities as a newly single parent of your special-needs child.

1. _____

2. _____

3. _____

4. _____

5. _____

Actual Steps

With all the transitions that occur when a family divides, usually the greatest concern parents have is how the breakup will affect their children.

Providing Continuity: The Smiths' Story

Brian Smith, now 7, had received a diagnosis of ASD with significant behavioral issues at the age of 4. When Brian's parents announced their separation and decision to divorce, they anticipated that Brian may have difficulty understanding and accepting the changes in their family. The previous year, Brian had been suspended twice for kicking his aide. The first time, he had a behavioral outburst over an unexpected math quiz, and the second time, he went into sensory overload after a music assembly. He didn't always react well to change.

Brian also had a 9-year-old sister, Emma. Even though the Smiths knew that the news of their separation could be difficult for the children to understand and accept in the beginning, Mrs Smith was more concerned about how the changes in their family would affect both children over time. First and foremost, the Smiths wanted their children to understand that their decision to divorce had nothing to do with either one of them. To that end, as suggested by their family therapist, Mr and Mrs Smith agreed to have a family meeting to explain to their children some (age-appropriate) practical and logistical details about their divorce.

"My husband and I realized that 'spelling out' for the kids when they would be with which parent was imperative. Knowing this in advance really helped them. Our goal was to be as unambiguous as possible about our new schedules and any other future expectations. Because routine was especially important in addressing Brian's needs, creating visual family schedules and laying out plans were crucial," Mrs Smith added.

During their separation process, the Smiths consulted with their family therapist regularly. The therapist helped them develop a "game plan" during their time of transition. For example, to make the transition smoother for both children, the therapist suggested that Mr and Mrs Smith inform Brian and Emma's schoolteachers about their new family circumstances. They also informed Brian's service providers immediately.

"Initially, I felt embarrassed about telling the school about our family's business, because I felt it was private. Then, I realized it would eventually become common knowledge anyway,"

Mrs Smith confided. "Emma did exhibit some social anxiety at school after my husband and I separated, so I was glad I spoke to her teachers about it ahead of time. Because they knew what was going on, they were understanding with Emma and were able to better address her anxiety at school. I feel it was the right decision to alert her teachers about our family's changing circumstances," she said.

As advised by their family therapist, the Smiths filled both of their homes with several of their children's favorite things—Legos and Transformers toys for Brian and games and books for Emma. Additionally, to address Brian's special diet and medication requirements, Mr and Mrs Smith provided gluten-free foods and Brian's special medications in both homes at all times.

"We made some very simple accommodations that were so important for the well-being of both of our children," said Mr Smith.

Although at times there were significant ups and downs between Mr and Mrs Smith both during and after their divorce, both parents were deliberate in their attempts to communicate openly and candidly with each other when it involved their children. All in all, the concessions they made for their children had a positive effect on how Brian and Emma were able to adjust during the transition. With all of the supports the Smiths put into place, even Brian was able to adjust as well as could be expected.

Take Actual Steps Forward _____

Provide a Stable Environment for You and Your Child

When you feel safe and secure, so will your child. Providing a loving, stable, and consistent environment for your special-needs child is vital. Help your child understand as much as possible that, despite the change in your relationship with the child's other parent, his or her relationship with each of you will remain the same. All children want to feel nurtured and protected, but children with autism may need additional reassurance and attention during this transitional period. Remember that the parents set the tone in the home. Try and establish a balance between structure and flexibility in your home(s).

TIP Giving reassurance and support during any significant transition is important. But, the change in your family unit will be a huge adjustment for your child with autism. Thus, generating extra attention, affection, and "special time" with your child is essential. Children with autism have difficulty with transition, and this is magnified when their home life is altered or a change has been made to their schedule. Support and nurture your child by extending story time, playing his or her favorite game, or baking something together. Be extra patient, more flexible, and especially loving with your child right now. Tell and show your child that he or she is loved, safe, and secure with you. Pay extra attention to your child's routines, and embrace his or her little idiosyncrasies. Transitioning is a process! And remember—*strive for improvement, not perfection.*

Transitional Support: Teddy as a Toddler

When my husband and I first separated, I recognized early on that Teddy, who had difficulty with transitions as a toddler, required extra time to get ready whenever we left the house. Whether we were running errands or just going for a walk,

Teddy needed time to transition to the next activity. Although I routinely gave him 5- and 10-minute warnings before any change occurred, I eventually realized that Teddy transitioned better if he could carry a transition item (of his choice) with him. At the time I came up with the idea, his transition item was a little blue "Thomas the Tank Engine" toy. It fit perfectly in his little palm.

Even though Teddy misplaced his transition toy on numerous occasions, which caused quite a conundrum in our household, I was prepared (or so I thought). Being the brilliant and ever-ready mother that I am, I decided to purchase five of those engines (which looked identical), and I stashed them in my purse for the times when we needed to dash out somewhere quickly but the original engine was nowhere to be found. Unfortunately, my son, who is also quite brilliant, knew instantly (I'm not sure how—they were all EXACTLY the same) that none of my backup blue engines could ever be mistaken for his original blue engine! I tried …

Be Open with Your Children about Your New Circumstances

When the decision has been made to split up your family unit, explaining this to your special-needs child can be disconcerting at first. Oftentimes, a professional who is familiar with ASD can help sort out specific family issues and/or provide strategies that can help you and your child process and receive this information better. Your child's routines and schedules will definitely change because of your split. This will make it necessary for you to explain to your child in advance the alterations that may occur. Sharing this important information may not happen in one conversation, but you might explain it to your child over time, in numerous conversations. This may also be an effective way to help your other children (without autism) understand what is happening. Either way, your child's transition will be easier if he or she knows what to expect in advance. Every child is different, so depending on your child's age and his or her ability to understand, when you feel it's appropriate, share this information with your child carefully and thoughtfully.

TIP Explaining your new circumstances to your special-needs child may be difficult. Having this conversation in a quiet setting, where he will feel most comfortable asking questions and/or expressing himself, would be best. (An example would be talking to him at home or on a walk together.) Give him details and answer his questions concisely. Share any pertinent and appropriate information that you feel will lessen your child's anxiety, fear, or anger.

Some children on the autism spectrum are just quiet by nature. The world could be falling down around them, and they might not react. That's not to say they are not affected or that they don't feel the pain of a tragedy. Instead, they may internalize what they perceive as emotional turmoil and family conflict. Those are the children who may need to be prompted, by asking about their thoughts and feelings concerning your new family circumstances. Depending on your child's age and cognitive ability, this will require finesse.

Conversely, you may have a child who asks hard and recurring questions about your new family division and what to expect. Try to be as patient and understanding as possible when explaining your family situation. Be clear. Clarify for her what is happening—don't justify the decision for your new circumstances. As you already know, many children with autism are extremely literal. So, using figurative language like "break apart," "breaking up," "broken," "splitting up," or even "separating" to describe your new family situation can be taken literally by a child with autism. You know your child best. If this may be the case, try to use words that are honest, pertinent, and clear. Describe your situation with sensitivity, without causing her any unnecessary anxiety due to the language you use. This can be tricky, but it's important to deliver your message with clarity.

Maintain Consistency in Your Child's Daily Activities, Routines, and Schedules

As often as possible, provide consistency regarding your child's routines, activities, and daily schedules. It's important for your child to be able to rely on his daily routine with as much regularity as possible. With so much of his family life altered because of your marital or relationship change, the least amount of disruption is best. Your child may have meltdowns, overreact, and/or behave in a manner that is unexpected or inappropriate at the slightest change in his routine. Remember to be patient and understanding with him. His life will be different, and the changes will be new. He too needs time to adjust to his new circumstances. The unknown can be frightening—perhaps even terrifying at times—and your child's actions may be reflected in his conduct at school and/or at home.

Be tolerant! For example, many children with autism can literally erupt at the slightest change in their everyday routines. When there is a divorce, add to the mix a new home environment, having to move back and forth between parents throughout the week and on the weekends, and learning the expectations (and there will be new ones) from each parent.

Think about it. Your child will have to navigate new surroundings, new expectations, and the adjustments that go along with having single parents living in separate homes. Holidays, birthdays, and everyday life will be different than before. This is a huge adjustment for any child, much less a child with autism! For some children with autism, it can take days and even weeks to recover from the smallest disruption in their routine. Things like having similar toys, books, and furnishings in both homes can help, but your child may reject even those things because they are not the same.

Having to adhere to a strict new visitation schedule may not be easy. It's new and different and can change from day to day. For a child who has transition challenges, this can be extremely difficult to adjust to. Allowing your child time to acclimate herself to the new circumstances takes time and understanding. Be patient with your child. New routines can be hard for anyone to adjust to.

TIP Maintain consistency for your child at home after your divorce. For example, if dinnertime has always been at 6 o'clock and you always read a story before bed, try and abide by these same routines. Maintaining the same structure in a new situation helps with continuity in your child's life at a time when everything else is changing.

Inform Your Children's School, Doctors, and Service Providers about Your Recent Changes

It is difficult to predict how your child may react to the change in your family unit. Emotions and attitudes may be heightened, and, as a result, your child's basic conduct may be uncharacteristically different. Thus, providing pertinent information that can be useful to those who relate to and work with your child on a regular basis may be helpful. Given the opportunity, children will often prefer to discuss their feelings about personal family issues with non–family members with whom they  have a bond, such as a psychologist, teacher, counselor, or behaviorist. Many of these professionals may have established a history with your child and are likely to provide him with the appropriate counsel, guidance, and understanding he needs. It's important to encourage your child to express his feelings to whomever he's most comfortable with.

Conversely, despite the change in your family unit, your child may react by not reacting at all. This behavior should also be addressed appropriately and with the proper professionals.

Sharing Is Important: Kyla's Story

Kyla's parents would describe her as a bubbly, bright, and chatty 10-year-old. Even though she received a diagnosis of Asperger's syndrome when she was 9, Kyla was uncharacteristically sociable. Her teachers knew her to be outgoing and friendly. When her parents announced their divorce unexpectedly, however, Kyla was devastated. Her disposition seemed to change overnight, and suddenly she had nothing to say—at least to her parents, anyway. If her mother asked Kyla about what happened at school, Kyla gave one-word answers. When her father spent time with Kyla on the weekends, she was sullen and reclusive. Kyla's parents were worried about her, and they asked her teachers to keep an eye on her at school. Kyla's math teacher, Mrs Greene, noticed that Kyla often sat alone at lunch and aimlessly walked the perimeter of the playground during recess.

One day, Mrs Greene asked Kyla if she could join her at lunch. Reluctantly, Kyla agreed. She asked to join her again the next day, and the day after that—and soon, Kyla welcomed the company. Eventually, Kyla opened up and revealed her anxiety about her parents' divorce. She explained to Mrs Greene how fearful she was about her new living situation. She talked about her dad's new apartment and described how her new bedroom was a loft—not even a bedroom with a door. She also shared how her mom had to return to work to pay the bills, and, as a result, Kyla had to wait at a neighbor's house after school until her mom got home from work. Her life had completely changed—affecting where she lived, what time she ate dinner, where she did her homework, and when she went to bed. Nothing was the same, and it was too much for Kyla to handle.

NOTE: Ultimately, Mrs Greene shared this information with Kyla's parents, and they made immediate adjustments (with Kyla's input) to help reduce and even eliminate her anxiety about all of the transitional changes.

> **TIP** Convey your current family circumstances (in writing or in person) to the people and professionals that interact with your special-needs child regularly. Ask them to report to you and/or your ex regarding any relevant physical, emotional, behavioral, and/or psychological changes involving your child as a result of your changing family situation.

Access Government Support and Services Available to Single Parents with Autistic or Special-Needs Children

Becoming a single parent is difficult, and it can be especially difficult when you have a special-needs child. Oftentimes, a newly single parent may feel unprepared to address the additional challenges that accompany raising a child on the autism spectrum. Depending on your unique circumstances, you may become eligible for public assistance programs that provide funding for basic necessities, along with additional supports for your special-needs child. Typically, eligibility for these resources can be based on financial and/or health needs.

TIP Many federal programs are specifically designed to allocate funds and services to children with ASD, as well as to single parents with special-needs children. Additionally, depending on the state where you reside, other programs may be available.

What Are Your Actual Steps Forward?

Write down the actual steps forward that will help you focus primarily on your child, his special needs, and the structure your child will need to ensure continued growth and development during this process.

1. _____

2. _____

3. _____

4. _____

5. _____

CHAPTER 2:
Co-Parenting Effectively in Two Homes

Single Parenting Is Done Effectively Over Time, Not Overnight

Divorce can be painful, even when it's amicable. The divorce rate for families with special-needs children is shockingly high. Raising a child on the autism spectrum as a single parent is a difficult prospect. Single moms and dads have raw emotions to deal with, and feelings of blame, fear, worry, and depression are par for the course. Many are working parents, which creates an entirely different set of additional challenges. Not only must a parent juggle the regular responsibilities of work and home, but he or she must also handle the unexpected but critical responsibilities inherent to caring for a child with a disability. When it comes to a child with autism, transitions are an issue in general. As a parent, you'll want to ensure that the transitional process involved in establishing two households will unfold with the least amount of emotional stress possible. To do so, this process should be considered carefully and well planned out. Preparing your child for this type of change in advance is essential.

Emerge from the Chaos into the Calm ——

Even if parents agree to share joint custody of their special-needs child, special circumstances and logistical considerations will play a role. Although every child is different, how your child deals with the separation and adjustment of his family unit and all that's involved will depend on a number of factors. Most commonly, an issue of concern is any modification in her routine. Outbursts may occur as a manifestation of the fear, agitation, anxiety, or anger she feels in response to the unfamiliar changes in her new circumstances.

Changes at School _____

Many children with autism
receive some type of specialized
education plan, in addition to
specific therapeutic interventions. If the goal is to maintain
consistency of these specialized
ASD programs for your child
with the least amount of disruption, parents must consider
all the variables when making
custody decisions that will affect

them. Questions to consider when deciding who will
have primary or physical child custody include: Do
both parents work outside the home? Whose schedule is
more flexible? Do both parents reside in the same town?
What's the distance between the two households? Can
both parents get their special-needs child to school and
maintain regular therapeutic appointments? Do finances play a role?

Agreeing to Agree in the Best Interest of Your Child

To co-parent effectively, child custody, child support, and the division of responsibilities need to be negotiated in the best interest of your child. If you are unable to devise an appropriate child-visitation schedule or have difficulty reaching a mutual agreement regarding child custody, this can be determined by a family-law judge in the county where you reside. Although formal custody agreements are often necessary, they leave little ability for the parents themselves to determine the outcome. Knowing that this outcome could prevail, "agreeing to agree" in the best interest of your child should be your plan of action.

Once certain aspects of co-parenting are determined, the overall experience for you and your child can eventually become a positive one. The aspects I'm referring to include custody, visitation schedules, division of holidays and vacation time, financial support (alimony, child support, special-education support, and ASD therapeutic services), medical and dental insurance coverage, and any other additional provisions a child with autism needs until he reaches adulthood. An example I can share is one Mother's Day when my son was little. It was my ex's weekend to have Thomas, but because it was Mother's Day, I wanted him to be with me. Although it would initially disrupt our ongoing visitation schedule, my ex ultimately agreed to give me the "extra" weekend, with the intent that I would reciprocate in a similar situation.

Another example was when Thomas was in third grade. According to his IEP, Thomas was receiving occupational therapy 1 hour per week at school. However, I felt he would benefit from an additional hour each week from an independent occupational therapist, which cost $65 an hour. My ex believed this was a waste of money. Because I felt strongly that the additional therapy would help Thomas, I decided to pay for the extra hour a week myself. Thus, I got what I felt was necessary for Thomas, and it cost my ex nothing. Problem solved.

Are You the Good Cop or the Bad Cop? _____

The needs of children with ASD can be countless and constant. Trying to find the balance between being the sole disciplinarian and the overly indulgent parent can be tough. Avoid being the "Disneyland parent," making the other parent act as the sole disciplinarian. This can cause your child to become confused and frustrated about what's expected of him and how he should respond. Don't give in to your child's every whim, and, conversely, don't overreact needlessly when he misbehaves or does something out of character.

Although I think I can promise that some days will be easier than others, try to create an environment that is structured and predictable for your child. Remember that you are in charge. Turn your new circumstances into an opportunity to establish and reinforce old rules, expectations, and consequences for your child and your household. For example, when you're trying to make dinner and your child is complaining about having to get off the computer because it's homework time, don't give in to him to make the complaining stop. Instead, give him a 5- or 10-minute warning before it's time to get off the computer, and really follow through with your request.

Outsmart Your Picky Eater

Many children on the autism spectrum have food texture issues and may have a reputation for being "picky eaters," either because they have a tactile problem or because they are resistant to trying anything new. This may make it difficult for their parents to provide them with a nutritious and balanced diet. Unfortunately, this issue often becomes more problematic when a child splits his time between two homes. Because dual households offer different foods, working as a team with your ex would be optimal. Share information with your child's other parent about his food issues, past and present. If he's skipping lunches at school, find out why. If she eats better at one home versus the other, find out why.

Communicating tips and ideas about how to create healthy and nutritional alternatives for your child is the goal.

Five Steps to Creating a Balanced Diet

1. *Add supplements to the menu.*
   If your child can't swallow a pill, buy chewable supplements. Some vitamins and minerals come in fruity flavors and various animal shapes. Some come in powdered form, which can be mixed in with your child's favorite beverage.

2. *Embrace what grows organically.*
   Some children are sensitive, have allergies, and react better to foods that are grown organically. These foods are typically processed without the use of insecticides, antibiotics, and chemical fertilizers, while other foods are grown with conventional or processed methods.

3. *Avoid food battles with your picky eater.*

   Choose your food battles carefully. When it comes to mealtimes with your child, not every vegetable or piece of fruit is worth fighting over. Making sure your child eats a balanced meal is a work in progress. If she skips a protein, fruit, or vegetable at lunch, offer one at dinner. If you can't get her to eat a certain type of food, try something similar, perhaps with a different texture, color, consistency, or flavor.

4. *Try to introduce one new food to your child's menu each week.*

   Make it fun! Explore new foods with your child, not in spite of her. Be creative. If you have a small child, let her choose a new color of food each week. Then, take her to the grocery store with you and let her find healthy foods in that color! Examples might be green spinach or broccoli, red apples or strawberries, yellow bananas or squash, and orange carrots and bell peppers.

5. *Let your child pick the menu.*

   Enlist your child in the preparation process. Pick a theme! If it's Italian night, make a homemade pizza together. If it's Mexican night, make chicken fajitas! Make a plan to choose a recipe, write a grocery list, and go to the market to buy your ingredients. Together with your child, prepare, cook, serve, and enjoy the meal as a family. Most ingredients can also be found with gluten- and casein-free options.

Keeping Schedules and Routines in Check in Two Homes

An important part of establishing stability in dual homes is having predictable schedules and routines that your child can rely on. Maintaining structure and consistency will eliminate unnecessary anxiety and worry. Children need certainty. Depending on your child's age and cognitive understanding, it's best to tell your child in advance what his schedule for the day and routine for the week will be. Whenever possible, have an open dialogue and be accessible to answer any questions or concerns he might have. You may even want to create visual reminders. For example, you can post lists, charts, or daily schedules about upcoming plans in common areas of the house so your child will see them. If it will relieve his anxiety, display daily food menus, weekly visitation schedules, and homework and chore charts for him. Make sure the information is clearly visible and within reach so he knows what's going on at all times. Let him take his charts and/or schedules with him when he is with the other parent, so he can keep on track.

Establish a Bedtime Ritual

Maintain a bedtime ritual for your child. An example would be brushing teeth, putting on pajamas, and then getting into bed for story time. If your child is a visual learner and you find that it's helpful for him to check off each bedtime task, make a "bedtime checklist" and tape it to his bedroom wall.

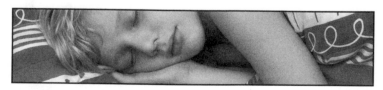

BEDTIME

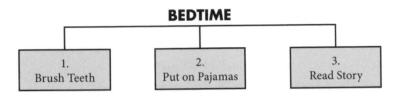

| 1. Brush Teeth | 2. Put on Pajamas | 3. Read Story |

Figure 1. You can make charts like this "bedtime checklist"
to help your child complete tasks from start to finish.

Figure 2 is a sample chore chart that you and your children can create and follow. I have found that when you include your children in this process, they are more invested in making it work. For example, let them make the chart and choose the time and chore they prefer. Chores and charts can alternate monthly. Let your children be in charge.

	Monday	*Wednesday*	*Friday*
JUSTIN	Makes bed before school	Feeds dog before school	Sets table before dinner
SARAH	Makes bed before school	Takes out the trash	Folds laundry after school
MOM	Makes breakfast for the family	Makes dinner for the family	Does the dishes

Figure 2. An example of a family chore schedule.

Busy schedules can be complicated and hard for any child to remember. Visual prompts are nice reminders of what will happen throughout your child's day and week. Oftentimes, a child with autism likes to know in advance what to expect during the school day. Figure 3 is an example of a weekly school schedule that includes logistical information, as well as special-education services for a child with autism.

PLAN B: Empowering the Single Parent, to Benefit Their Child with Autism

	Occupational Therapy	Speech Therapy	Social-Skills Group	Assistive Technology
MONDAY	4 PM: Mom drives Justin and picks him up afterward			
TUESDAY		5 PM: Dad drives Justin and picks him up afterward		
WEDNESDAY				12:30 PM: Justin goes to Ms Smith's room at school
THURSDAY			2:45 PM: Carpool drives Justin and Dad picks him up afterward	
FRIDAY	1:30 PM: Justin goes to multi-purpose room at school with Mr Jones			
SATURDAY			11:30 AM: Dad drives Justin and Mom picks him up afterward	

Figure 3. A sample visual agenda for Justin's therapies.

Children like to be "in the know." This is especially true for a child with autism. Knowing what to expect alleviates anxiety and creates predictability. Figure 4 is a chart that provides "the who, what, and when" as it relates to a child's visitation schedule.

SUNDAY	Kids are with Dad until 5 PM
MONDAY	Kids are with Mom all day
TUESDAY	Kids are with Mom all day
WEDNESDAY	Kids are with Dad from 5 PM until Thursday morning at 8 AM
THURSDAY	Kids are with Mom all day
FRIDAY	Kids are with Dad starting at 5 PM
SATURDAY	Kids are with Dad all day

Figure 4. A sample visitation chart for Justin and Sarah, for the week of January 9-15.

As your child gets older, it's good to instill a sense of independence. One way to accomplish this is to have him or her create a personal schedule or weekly planner, like the one in Figure 5. It's a good way to establish responsibility.

	Samantha	Justin	Mom and/or Dad
MONDAY	School play		Mom and Dad attend school play
TUESDAY	Math test	Spelling test	
WEDNESDAY			
THURSDAY	School field trip		Dad chaperones field trip
FRIDAY		Class art auction	Mom brings cupcakes

Figure 5. Your child can create a visual schedule of weekly school activities and events.

As a single parent, your schedule may vary from week to week. It is easy to create a weekly schedule that works well for you and your children, like the one in Figure 6. Let your child fill in her own tasks and appointments.

	Child 1	Child 2	Parent
MONDAY	Task/ appointment	Task/ appointment	Task/ appointment
TUESDAY	Task/ appointment	Task/ appointment	Task/ appointment
WEDNESDAY			
THURSDAY			
FRIDAY			

Figure 6. A simple schedule like this one can be useful for everyone in the family to refer to.

Simple Solutions for Keeping Both Parents "on the Same Page" ————————

Keeping abreast of your child's school agenda can be difficult to do. Things like tests, report cards, field trips, parent-teacher conferences, and other school events can be overwhelming and hard to remember. It's best to establish a cooperative relationship with your child's teacher, principal, and service providers at school. Encourage

your child's teacher to maintain regular communication with both parents, perhaps by phone or e-mail. Also, always request that both parents receive copies of school announcements, progress reports, and report cards. Be certain that your child's school has both parents' current contact information, especially in case of an emergency.

Try and stay on the same page with your ex about what school activities or obligations are coming up. Offer quick reminders to one another, whenever possible. Remember, it only benefits your child to have both parents supportive of him and his activities. Sharing information with your child's other parent is an important part of co-parenting. Whether your child has the lead role in the school play, is failing algebra, or is biting other kids at recess, informing each other about your child's progress (or lack of progress) is important.

○ Emotional Steps Forward _____

Co-parenting can be tough—period! Creating boundaries, realistic expectations of each other, and a reasonable division of parenting responsibilities takes commitment and patience.

Working It Out: Rachel and Danielle's Story

When she became a single parent, Rachel was able to see early on that co-parenting effectively with her ex was the ultimate goal. As challenging as it could be at times, co-parenting was in the best interest of her children. Growing up in a single-parent home herself, Rachel could identify with many emotions her children were experiencing during and after the split with her ex. As a result, Rachel and her ex established "ground rules" that were important to both of them.

Both children were in high school when Rachel and the kids moved out of the family home. Their son, Eli, was an honor-roll student and a senior in high school. Their daughter Danielle was a freshman in high school and excelled in art. Danielle received a diagnosis of ASD when she was in the third grade, but she had been progressing extremely well thanks to a number of outside academic and social supports over the years.

Rachel and her ex agreed that the children's time would be split evenly between both homes, as would the parental responsibilities, including homework assistance, school projects, extracurricular activities, and rides to and from events and activities. Rachel and her ex loved their children very much and worked extremely hard to co-parent them successfully. Initially, both children seemed to accept their family's division well. A year later, however, when school became increasingly rigorous for Danielle, she began having frequent meltdowns at school and at home. Eventually, Danielle began isolating herself from others. This concerned her parents greatly. Consequently, her other family members began attending family therapy sessions with her (including Eli). It was especially important for Danielle to undergo counseling in a neutral setting, where she could express and discuss her feelings about her parents' breakup, as well as the growing pressure she felt at school—both socially and academically.

It wasn't long before a plan was developed to address Danielle's immediate issues. It was determined that she needed more social opportunities with peers, as well as tutoring from Eli in algebra and biology. Equally important was attending family therapy. Coincidentally, therapy proved to be a great platform for Eli to communicate his plans for his future.

"First and foremost, we are a united front," Rachel would often say. "My ex and I have made a 'deal' to agree to disagree when a resolution is not possible. It's the most fundamental ingredient of co-parenting effectively," offered Rachel.

♡ Take Emotional Steps Forward _____

Develop Clear Boundaries When Co-Parenting as a Team

In the best interest of your child, try to engage in cooperative (if not friendly) interactions with your ex about
your child. Although you have severed your relationship
as a couple, hopefully you can still maintain a "co-parenting" approach when raising your child with autism.
Establish clear visitation boundaries between the two of
you. Don't find excuses to drop in on your ex and your
child. Don't show up unannounced to see your child at
school because you suspect that your ex hasn't packed
a nutritious lunch or dressed your child appropriately.
And, if you are the parent on the other side of these
antics, don't allow it. This "unpredictable" behavior will
only confuse your child. Instead, try to communicate
openly with your ex on a regular basis to confirm the details and logistics of the agreed-upon visitation schedule.

Keep in mind that it benefits the entire family to
uphold the arranged visitation regime. If you find that

the shared custody schedules you've legally agreed upon have become unrealistic for you, your ex, or your child (for whatever reason), try to come to an alternate and mutually agreed-upon schedule that will support your child's best interests.

TIP If the goal is to co-parent effectively, a legal, shared custody agreement specifying who has your child when, with defined dates and times, must be reached and respected by both parents. For example, if your agreement says you have your child Wednesdays from 6 PM until 8 AM the following morning and every other weekend for 48 hours at a time, abide by that schedule. If you've requested to call your child on the telephone every evening at 7:30 to say goodnight, abide by that schedule. If your agreement says your child alternates weekends with you, abide by that schedule!

NOTE: Not all relationships end well. If you are unable to maintain an amicable relationship with your ex initially, understand that bad feelings often improve, and wounds can heal over time (hopefully). When that simply cannot occur, focus on parenting to the best of your ability and moving on.

Have Realistic Expectations Regarding the Division of Responsibilities

Managing your child's routines, schedules, and appointments can be hectic, particularly when there are two homes. Whenever possible, try to work as a team when it comes to supporting your child(ren). Between extra-curricular activities and special-education programs and interventions, balancing the logistics and maintaining your child's appointments can become a full-time job. The division of parental responsibilities when you have a child with autism requires organization, time management, and commitment from all involved. Whether your child attends school for part of the day or the full day, determining the division of responsibilities and creating a "schedule" in advance for both parents to refer to is critical. When therapies are involved, such as psychotherapy, occupational therapy, speech therapy, Applied Behavioral Analysis, and social-skills therapy, this is especially important. A clear understanding, in which each parent's agreed-upon role is defined, will eliminate unnecessary confusion and frustration for both parents and especially for your child.

TIP Whenever possible, maintain your commitments and agreements regarding the division of parental responsibilities. If you've agreed to take your child to his speech therapy appointment every Monday afternoon at 4 o'clock, as well as "friendship group" every Thursday evening at 6 o'clock, stick to that schedule. If, on occasion, you realize that you unexpectedly have a schedule conflict and you can't abide by the schedule you've agreed to, communicate your situation to your ex immediately and come up with a "Plan B." Together, perhaps you can resolve the issue without further complicating the matter and/or having it affect your child. And if you're the parent on the other end of that scenario, try to accept the unexpected change without confrontation (adopt a "Plan B" attitude).

Present a United Front

I can't stress enough that parental teamwork is ideal. Children with ASD seek predictability and consistency. By presenting a united front, your child will quickly recognize the fundamental structure in both homes, which will create a much-needed sense of security for him. Providing a loving and nurturing home includes establishing rules, as well as appropriate discipline and consequences. This is especially important for children on the autism spectrum, who can tend to feel fearful, anxious, sad, or even depressed. When both parents work together, the better the child will feel about his new circumstances. If that is simply impossible, try to be cordial to one another. Don't undercut the other parent's efforts in front of your child. It's always best to communicate with each other directly or through attorneys if necessary—but never use your child to communicate with your ex. Your child should not ever be the "go-between" for you or your ex, regarding any issue. Period!

TIP Even when you don't appreciate, respect, or like something the other parent has said to or done with your child, try (very hard) not to share those feelings with your child. Instead, discuss the issue directly with your ex, if for no other reason than to attempt to recognize his or her view when it comes to your child. It may be better to approach this in writing so you can contemplate your response carefully.

Agree to Disagree

Do your best to consult, discuss, confer, and collaborate with your ex with regard to your special-needs child. Ultimately, the goal is to parent your child effectively in a secure and loving environment. Parents won't always agree on issues that involve their child, and this is not to be expected. In such situations, conflict is sometimes

inevitable, and resolutions are often impossible. It happens. Recognize it for what it is and move on. Perhaps you can revisit the issue another time (or not). However, if the issue is important enough, perhaps you may need to seek conflict resolution from a professional or from the justice system.

TIP Try not to undermine, challenge, or sabotage the efforts of the other parent, even when you disagree with (or dislike) him or her. If it happens that you simply do not agree with a decision, action, or situation regarding your child, just "agree to disagree." Don't expend any extra energy on the issue—it's not worth the emotional drain. Chances are, nothing will change except the way you communicate with your ex. Just move on. Do this for yourself, your emotional well-being, and your child. It's a new chapter! Turn the page.

Devote Quality Time to Your Child When You're Together

When families separate, the dynamics change. Whatever role you played prior to your split may significantly change during and/or after your family division. Whether you were a stay-at-home parent or worked 60 hours a week, when parental roles shift, your child may feel confused by the change. Try and devote quality time to your child when you have her with you. Use that special time to focus on just her.

TIP Something as easy as helping your child with her homework, assisting her with a school project, or enjoying a peanut butter sandwich is valuable time spent together. Other examples include playing board games, finger-painting, and making homemade brownies. On sunny days, you could plant a vegetable garden, visit the park or beach, or dig for worms in your backyard. Whatever you do with your child, make new memories and have fun doing it. It's important for her to know that she is safe, secure, and loved by both parents. Although your child with autism may have more special needs than your other children (if you have more than one), dividing time and attention equally between your children is paramount.

When it's your weekend with your child, share some quality time by making something together—like cookies! Let your child be in charge, while you assist her for this project. The goal is to have fun!

☾ Practical Steps

Life is unpredictable. When the unexpected happens, we often find that we are more unprepared than we'd ever imagined. As a practical matter, it's always good to have a "Plan B" discussion with the other parent about "what if" situations that may arise for your family, especially if you have a child with autism.

No Warning: Amanda and Mark's Story

Amanda was devastated when her husband Steve died suddenly from a heart attack at the age of 52. To make ends meet, Amanda and her two children—Mark, aged 12, and Jim, aged 15—were forced to move into town with Amanda's elderly mother. Having lived outside of town in a rural Midwestern area, Amanda had homeschooled her boys from elementary through middle school. Amanda and Steve had been happy living away from the hustle and bustle of downtown.

But, when Mark received a diagnosis of autism and demonstrated limited verbal skills at the age of 3, access to appropriate educational programs was logistically challenging. The therapeutic services Mark received were therefore limited. After Steve's death and the new move, the boys entered public school for the first time. Mark began receiving on-site special-education services at school, such as small-group speech

---

therapy and one-on-one occupational therapy. Both therapies honed in on his special needs. Mark also began receiving individual psychotherapy to deal with his feelings about his father's sudden absence.

Steve's unexpected death was a devastating loss for the entire family, on a number of levels. Because Steve had handled all of the family's finances, Amanda had no knowledge of their monthly income, expenses, or outstanding debt, which turned out to be significant.

"Our financial predicament, coupled with the emerging transitional challenges that my boys were experiencing in their new environment, were overwhelming for me," Amanda confessed.

Both boys were outwardly struggling with having to adapt to a new home, a new school, and new peers. While Mark seemed noticeably uncomfortable with new people and surroundings, Jim had extreme difficulty with accepting his father's unexpected death and dealing with the changes in his everyday life. Amanda was aware of Jim's anxiety and took him to a grief-counseling group for teens.

Adjusting to all the changes and having to become an instant single parent was difficult for Amanda. "I knew the recovery period would be a process for me and my boys. I also knew that the task of addressing Mark's ongoing autism-related issues would be daunting," Amanda said.

Eventually, Amanda joined an autism parent support group in town, where she sought guidance and emotional support from other parents of kids with ASD.

☀ Take Practical Steps Forward _____

Establish Structure in the Home

A surefire way to help prevent your child's meltdowns, breakdowns, or rebellious behavior is to create an atmosphere filled with structure, consistency, and predictability. Change is hard—especially for a child with autism. Whether your child rotates from one home to another or not, establishing structure helps provide a sense of stability for him. Allow your child to feel useful around the home. Perhaps he could set and clear the dinner table a couple of nights per week or fold towels on laundry day. Empower him by involving him. By setting up a structure and guidelines for him to follow, expectations will be better understood.

TIP Regardless of how or why you are in a single-parent situation, if you've requested that your child complete his homework before he plays his favorite video game or does a Lego activity, maintain that same expectation in your new home situation. If a "no television during the week" rule existed prior to your separation, continue that rule in your new home environment.

Dinnertime Is Family Time

Dinnertime is a time for bonding, sharing, and catching up with your child about everyday stuff. Mealtime can be a designated family activity where you and your child can express yourselves openly about the day's events. For children with autism, it's a great time to practice social exchanges in a safe atmosphere. Whatever time of the day you and your child convene as a family, whether it's at breakfast or dinner, encourage her to talk about her "plus" and "minus" moments. It's a great way to learn what's going on with your child and gives you an opportunity to offer guidance.

> **TIP** ▶ Whether it is Saturday-morning pancakes or Sunday-night burritos, designate "mealtime" as "family time." Once you've established this routine, you and your child will look forward to this special time together (believe it or not!).

Plan for the Unexpected, Because Things Change (in Both Homes)

When families separate into single-family households, they need to consider new obstacles that may affect their daily schedules. Child care is one of them. Children's schools have holidays, children get sick, appointments get cancelled, and often buses and carpools change without any notice. Things happen without warning every day, and parents need to have a  "Plan B" in place for these types of incidences. Develop a backup plan with your ex to address the unanticipated "what-if" situations that can occur with your child. This is especially critical for a child with autism who has a rigid mindset. For example, something unexpected that comes up, or a lack of predictability, could send a child on the autism spectrum straight into an emotional breakdown, whereas a typically developing child may just need to regroup before moving forward. For a single parent, it is critical to have a "Plan B" in place and to teach your rigid child with ASD that unexpected things happen in life. You may even want to practice (on the weekends) how to handle unexpected situations. When a problem occurs, teach your child how to be part of the solution. It's a skill they can learn—I promise you that!

TIP Compile a list of people that includes family, friends, and neighbors who are willing to help out with your child in case of an emergency. Share that list with your ex and your child's school. Make your child aware of your "Plan B" list so he is not completely surprised when and if it needs to be implemented. When appropriate, have your child carry several names and phone numbers from your "Plan B" list in his backpack.

Allow Time for Adjustments

Slow and steady wins the race. Don't expect things to change overnight. Any big life change takes time to adjust to. Regular routines, special traditions, and everyday practices are no longer the same. Your life has taken a different turn, just as it has for your special-needs child. Allow yourself, your ex, and your child time to process the change. Everyone reacts to change differently. This is especially true for children on the autism spectrum.

TIP Don't keep your feelings pent up inside! Find a safe outlet where you and/or your child can express yourselves openly about the way you feel. A school counselor, therapist, or family friend may be helpful—especially during the adjustment period when transitions are less predictable. Try to be patient and tolerant with yourself and your child during the hard times.

Prepare for the Future

Face it: Your life is different. And planning for a new future can be overwhelming financially, emotionally, and socially. Finding the balance is primary. This may be an opportunity to consider new aspirations, new goals, and new responsibilities, as well as address new concerns. Take a positive approach in planning your new future!

TIP Set a financial goal for yourself. Outline steps for how to achieve that goal. Keep track of your progress and obstacles. Improve your emotional state of being by reaching out to those who can assist you when you are feeling hopeless. Enrich your social experiences and networking opportunities by accepting invitations from friends, coworkers, or acquaintances for events, outings, and social activities.

Practical Parent-to-Parent Tips for Co-Parenting Effectively _____

1. *Maintain loving and healthy home environments.*
   Establish a harmonious way of life by valuing the other parent's efforts in front of your child.

2. *Reinforce stability in both homes.*
   Build a balanced, safe, and secure haven where your child feels comfortable.

3. *Respect your child's routines and schedules in both homes.*
   Try and coordinate specific schedules for necessities like occupational therapy, speech therapy, and psychotherapy. Don't forget to make in-home schedules

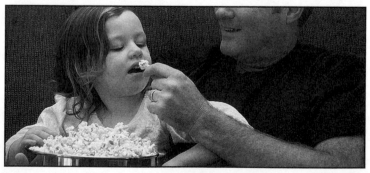

that take into account special diets, medications, mealtimes, bedtimes, and so on.

4. *Encourage family time in both homes.*
Engage with your child by playing games, organizing "pizza and movie" night, or maybe even watching programs on television that he enjoys.

5. *Provide consistency between your two households.*
Sit down with your child and create positive weekly charts, so he can focus on completing a task and feeling good about himself.

⚋ Actual Steps

Taking steps to actually change your circumstances, especially when it involves raising a special-needs child alone, takes guts. No matter what kind of single parent you are (mother, father, grandparent, guardian, foster parent, or relative), raising a child on the autism spectrum can be complicated, frustrating, and overwhelming at times.

Keep Searching for Answers: Mike's Story

After making partner in a successful accounting firm, Mike, who wasn't married, adopted 8-year-old Joshua through the foster care system. Mike's sister had worked in the system for years and knew Joshua personally. She often talked to Mike about Joshua, described his sweet nature, and touted his many talents.

"Joshua has a photographic memory and he can play the piano by ear. He seems to have almost perfect pitch, even though he's never had a piano lesson," Mike's sister said.

Because Joshua also exhibited some considerable behavioral issues, including rude outbursts, oppositional behavior and defiance, and a constant challenge of authority, a permanent foster placement was unsuccessful for him. That's when Mike agreed to adopt Joshua. After many evaluations and multiple interventions and therapies, Joshua began to improve rapidly. It wasn't until Joshua entered middle school that his grades started to slip. That's also when Mike noticed his social regression. More tests were undertaken, and the results indicated that Joshua had learning disabilities. He received diagnoses of dysgraphia (a deficiency in the ability to write, regardless of reading ability) and dyscalculia (an innate difficulty in learning or comprehending mathematics). He was also given a diagnosis of autism. It was then that Mike began his exploration into the world of autism to learn and discover more about how to best help Joshua. Supports for academic and social resources were the first two areas he addressed.

"Although I'm glad Joshua finally has a diagnosis and is getting the help he needs, I wish he had received a diagnosis when he was much younger," said Mike. "I think receiving early interventions could have made a real difference for Joshua and his development."

Take Actual Steps Forward ─────

Accept Change

Many of you will agree that the needs of children with autism are forever transforming. Put simply, their needs are different than those of typically developing children. As a result, they may require additional understanding, attention, and acceptance from their parents.

TIP When faced with a problem or dilemma, children with autism may react or respond in ways that are not typical. It doesn't matter if your child is verbal or not—encourage him to share his feelings (no matter what they are) by talking, writing them down or typing them out, drawing a picture, or even writing a story about what he's feeling.

Coordinate Regular Family Meetings So Your Child Can Express Thoughts, Feelings, and What She Is Experiencing

Children have emotions, reactions, and opinions just like the rest of us. If your special-needs child appears overly moody, sensitive, tearful, or angry, allow her to express these thoughts and feelings to you openly (however she does that best). This may often be difficult, as children with autism articulate their thoughts differently. Regardless, try and talk to her about how she feels and what she thinks. Discuss any struggles you've noticed she may be having. Inquire about what's happening at school, with her friends, or with any other issue you feel is affecting her. Create opportunities for her to open up with you and reveal her true emotions.

TIP During your family meetings, encourage your child to express any anxiety she might be experiencing about the unknown or unexpected. Welcome her questions about new circumstances or future plans, and ask her questions too. This gives her a platform to feel validated, while allowing her to practice her problem-solving skills with your guidance.

Encourage Your Children to Take on Responsibilities to Learn about and Demonstrate Independence

Let your child track her own personal progress at school and/or at home, when appropriate, and encourage her positive growth. Let her know you are proud of her ini-

tiative, sense of responsibility, and cooperation. When appropriate, allow your child to take part in the decision-making process for family issues. This bolsters her self-confidence and will help prepare her for independence.

And for heaven's sake, learn to delegate! It's important for both you and your child to feel valued and appreciated. This may be a perfect time to assign age-appropriate household tasks to your child with special needs. It's important to encourage her to be involved in the process of running the home.

> **TIP** Use a reward system (such as an allowance, free computer time, or special outings). Involve your child in making her own homework charts, chore charts, and meal charts. Commend her for her accomplishments. Praise her for her achievements and for completing her everyday tasks.

Enlist Your Child in Family Projects

Depending on your child's cognitive ability, attention span, and passion, select a project that she is interested in planning with you. Engaging her in this way will instill in her a sense of initiative, organizational skills, and self-confidence. It's a win-win for everyone!

TIP Whatever event you have coming up, make it a family affair. Recruit your children in activities like writing out the weekly grocery list, preparing the family meal, making the holiday cookies, folding laundry, planting a vegetable garden, organizing the next family camping trip, and budgeting a family excursion.

Create "Special Time" for You and Your Child

Show your child how important she is to you. Spend special time with her individually, doing something she enjoys. Make treats for a school function, share a special meal, read a story, play a card came, or engage in an activity that is "scheduled" for just you and your child. Both parents can enjoy "special time" in their respective homes.

TIP If you have more than one child, be sure to divide your time equally between your children, so no one feels left out. Living with a special-needs sibling can be overwhelming at times. A lot of the attention from parents is devoted to the child with the most immediate needs. Oftentimes, you can find support groups for siblings of a special-needs child in your community. It's important that your child without special needs receives support, too. Whenever possible, "divide and conquer" between households. If one parent is parenting one child, the other parent can spend special time with the other child(ren). Divide parental obligations, responsibilities, activities, and events between your children equally. For "special time," you could visit the library, go shopping, have lunch, take a hike, play cards, or make Rice Krispies treats with your child for her upcoming class party.

Every family is different. Concentrate on what will make you and your co-parent cooperate in the most cohesive and effective manner. List five strategies that will help you co-parent successfully and harmoniously in the best interests of your child(ren).

1. _____

2. _____

3. _____

4. _____

5. _____

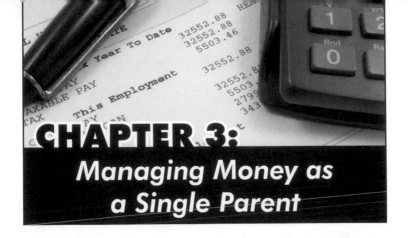

CHAPTER 3:
Managing Money as a Single Parent

An annual study by the U.S. Department of Agriculture indicates that for middle-income families with a child born in 2007, the costs of providing food, shelter, clothing, and other necessities will total $204,060 by the child's 18th birthday.*

Raising a child on the autism spectrum can cost exponentially more than that statistic. Whether you were the parent who handled the family finances or not, as a single parent of a special-needs child, maintaining a monthly budget is especially necessary. Many single parents of a child with autism have extra expenses. Household expenses may have shifted significantly, and, therefore, discretionary income (for both parents) may have virtually disappeared. If that's your scenario, smart shopping and better budgeting can be useful tools. Your child may require special support services, special foods, medications, and therapeutic services. Thus, prioritizing your budget should be your first plan of action as you develop your "Plan B."

☉ Develop a Plan of Action: Prioritize Needs and Wants _____

Start by totaling your monthly income from all sources, including employment, alimony, child support, and any other sources. Make two lists to create your monthly budget. Create a primary or "needs" list, as well as a secondary or "wants" list. You can look at both lists to help you prioritize your expenses. Start by deducting your mandatory expenses from your total income to determine the monthly balance you have left over. From that balance amount, choose expenses from your secondary list. (See Exercise 2.)

NOTE: Depending on your financial circumstances, many single parents may qualify for state and/or federal assistance programs designed specifically for families with special-needs children. These programs may include home health care, respite care, child care, food, housing, and possibly educational assistance.

EXERCISE 2: *Establishing Your Monthly Budget*

1. First, create a primary ("needs") list of mandatory expenses. It should look like this:

Primary List

Rent/mortgage _____   (Property taxes) _____

Food _____

Clothing _____

Health insurance _____   (Dental) _____

Car payment _____   (Car insurance) _____   (Gasoline) _____

Public transportation _____

Electricity _____   (Natural gas) _____

Garbage _____

Water/sewer _____

Phone _____

Homeowner's/renter's insurance _____

Income taxes _____

Other _____

Savings account balance _____

2. Write a secondary ("wants") list. It might look like this:

Secondary List

Cable _____

Internet _____

Cell phone _____

Retirement savings _____

Life insurance _____

Education costs _____

Children's extracurricular activities _____

Entertainment _____

Pet care _____

Personal care (haircuts, etc) _____

Babysitting/child care _____

Travel _____

Miscellaneous _____ (This could be stamps, newspapers, rented movies, toys, toll fees, donations, birthday/holiday gifts, etc)

3. Calculate your total monthly income and note that figure here:

Total monthly income: _____

4. Now, prioritize each item on your primary list on the basis of "need." Rearrange the items on your list accordingly, so you can see at a glance what's most important.

5. Prioritize each item on the secondary list on the basis of "want." Rearrange the items in this list in the same way you did for your priorities.

6. Select which secondary expenses you can afford, on the basis of how much income you have available after subtracting your primary expenses.

Autism-Related Expenses

Children with autism often benefit from many different services, depending on their age and needs. As an example, in Exercise 3, I have listed various services. While many services may improve your child's overall progress, your financial situation may preclude you from continuing to provide a particular service for a period of time.

⊙ Develop a Plan of Action: Prioritize Autism-Related Expenses _____

Prioritize the services you feel your child needs at any point in time. If necessary, modify or temporarily change your child's services to reflect your current budget and your child's greatest need. Example: If your child has been receiving speech therapy for 1 hour twice a week, ask if you can reduce the service to 1 hour once a week or break the sessions up into ½-hour sessions twice a week. As your budget improves over time, increase your child's services as needed. There is no rulebook to follow, and there is no wrong answer. Each situation is unique.

EXERCISE 3: *Autism-Related Expenses*

What are your current autism-related expenses? Use this worksheet to prioritize your monthly autism-related budget and expenses, so you can factor these expenses in with your primary and secondary lists of expenses.

Monthly Services

Speech therapy	_____	Child care	_____
Occupational therapy	_____	Respite	_____
Behavioral therapy	_____	Academic tutor	_____
Floortime	_____	Special vitamins	_____
Psychotherapy	_____	Minerals	_____
Social-skills therapy	_____	GF/CF foods	_____
Life coach	_____	Special summer camps	_____
Job coach	_____	After-school program	_____
Alternative medicine	_____	Advocate	_____
Special programs	_____	Special-ed attorney	_____
Other	_____	Extra	_____

Total monthly services expenses _____

Financial Checks and Balances_____

Once you've prioritized your total monthly living expenses, subtract those expenses from your monthly income (see Exercise 4). Note that your expenses may change over time, and as they do, you will need to adjust your finances accordingly. Single parents no longer have the luxury of shared financial responsibility for their family, and that reality can be daunting at times. However, financial security is attainable, regardless of your marital status or income level. By living within your means, making sound and reasonable financial decisions, and maintaining a well-organized budget, you too can achieve a healthy financial future.

EXERCISE 4: *Put It All Together*

Now put all the numbers together to see where you stand on your total monthly income and expenses. Remember, you can always make adjustments. You may need to reallocate money from one expense to another to make things work. We prioritized all three of your lists—primary, secondary, and autism-related expenses—just for this purpose.

Total monthly income _____

Total primary expenses _____

Total secondary expenses _____

Total autism-related expenses _____

Total monthly expenses _____

Saving on Autism-Related Services _____

There may be ways you can reduce the costs of the services your child receives. Here are some ideas to help you cut costs while maintaining services he or she may need.

1. *Ask if service fees are negotiable.*
   Always ask if your child's service provider has a sliding scale or summer/winter special programs. You might find that because business is often slower during these times (as families are away for vacation), it's the perfect time to negotiate program fees.

2. *Ask to shorten therapeutic sessions.*
   If you are having trouble continuing your child's services, rather than eliminating them altogether, ask your child's service provider if you can reduce the session time. Or, maybe you could go half as often.

3. *Investigate "two for the price of one."*
   You may know of a friend that could benefit from the same service your child is receiving. If so, ask your service provider if they'd be interested in

giving a "two for the price of one" deal. You may be able to split the cost with the other family.

4. *Compare health insurance policies to get the best price.*
Shop around to find out which health insurance companies have the best autism coverage as part of their plan. Look into new legislation—both state and federal programs—to make sure your health insurance company is following the latest relevant regulations. If they aren't, bring it to their attention. You can file a complaint in writing.

5. *Look into extended school year support services.*
If your child has an IEP and receives support services during the school year, such as speech and occupational therapy (as provided by your school district), find out if your child is eligible for these same services during the "extended school year" (aka the summer). If so, it's a service provided at no cost to you.

Single Parent–to–Single Parent Tips: Top 15 Money-Saving Strategies

1. *Buy generic when possible.*

   Don't get stuck on name brands. Whenever you can, buy non-labeled food items and generic prescription medications. Don't pay more for a name brand or label. Shop smart!

2. *Buy in bulk when practical.*

   Save money and stock up on your favorite foods and goods by buying in bulk. As a general rule, more is less when buying in volume. (However, don't get lured into buying fancy foods, prepared foods, or foods that you don't ordinarily eat.)

3. *Buy foods that are in season.*

   Fruits and vegetable are typically less expensive at farmers' markets, and you can often negotiate for a better price. (Barter, haggle, make it a game!)

4. ***Cook at home.***
   If you're living on a budget or trying to save money, cook at home. You'll save gas, time, and energy, and you'll get exactly what you ordered! (Think how much money you can save by skipping the tip when you eat in!)

5. ***Look for sales, coupons, and reduced prices whenever possible.***
   Look for grocery specials or store coupons on staple goods. Buying foods that are selling at a reduced price is always a great way to save money. Most markets have a weekly list of what food items are on sale. Sunday newspapers, cooking magazines, and food Web sites are another way to find coupons to save money.

6. ***Buy frozen foods.***
   They're well preserved and can be up to 35% less expensive than fresh foods.

7. *List, list, list—and stick to your shopping list at the store.*
   Don't let yourself get sidetracked with sale items for foods you don't ordinarily eat. Check your cupboards before you leave the house and only buy what's on your list!

8. *Never shop when you are hungry or rushed.*
   Shopping on a full stomach will limit any impulse buying and unnecessary purchases.

9. *Shop as needed.*
   It's better to shop more often and actually use what you buy, rather than shop less often and waste food that's gone bad.

10. *Pay attention to pricing by the unit.*
    Larger stores typically buy bulk items for less, meaning they can usually sell those items to you for less cost.

11. *Track your spending for one month.*
    If you find that you are over budget, examine
    where, what, why, and how it happened. Make the
    reduction(s) needed to stay within the budget you've
    designed for yourself and regroup. Start fresh the
    next month by staying within the guidelines you've
    given yourself.

12. *Pay yourself first.*
    To build up a reserve account (no matter how small),
    start by subtracting a percentage of your net income
    each month (whatever you can afford) and sock it
    away. Before you know it, you will have started a
    nice reserve account by "paying yourself first."

    NOTE: For convenience, you might consider auto-
    matically deducting 5% or 10% from your monthly
    paycheck and depositing it into a savings or money
    market account (whichever earns the most interest).

Total Gross Pay TD   128
Gross for Tax TD   12
Tax paid TD

13. *Try to use cash, not credit cards.*

Know what you are spending and saving at all times. If you are in credit card debt, pay off the highest-interest debt first. When possible, increase your payments to a level that chips away at your principal amount, while still allowing you to stay within your budget.

14. *Try not to pay interest—on anything—if you don't have to.*

To avoid paying interest, pay off your credit card debt on time and in full each month. If that's not possible, pay 10%-15% more than what is due each month. This will reduce your debt faster and keep your credit report in good standing.

15. *Sock away any "windfall" money.*

If you receive a tax return, inheritance, settlements, or any other unexpected windfall, sock it away for a rainy day! You never know when you'll have unexpected expenses, especially when it comes to your child with autism.

☀ Planning for the Future _____

I've often heard single parents of special-needs children say, "I can never die!" I can totally relate to this statement. Although all parents worry about what will happen to their children when they die, single parents who have a child on the autism spectrum are especially concerned about what will happen to their child after they're gone. So … what will happen to them? Where will they live? Although it may be hard for some of you to imagine now, if your children are really young, those with older children will want to know. Will their children be capable of employment and be able to support themselves? Will they require government assistance? And, if so, who will help guide them through that process? These agonizing questions often trouble the minds of many single parents raising children on the autism spectrum. However, the best way to address these natural concerns is to plan ahead. Plan now for the future and the future of your child! How? Establish a plan of action (your "Plan B").

How Do I Plan for the Future?

When you do finally pass away, who will replace you in your child's life? This is a very difficult question to answer, because you are irreplaceable! However, there will come a time when you will be gone, and your special-needs child will need to seek assistance from other people. So the best way to prepare for when that happens is to create a "Plan B." Plan ahead for what you want to happen to protect your child after you are gone. What if your child is young? Will she need a guardian? Will she need support? If so, how much? Do you think she'll be able to live independently when she reaches adulthood? Regardless of the value of your assets or the size of your estate, it's important to have an estate plan—especially for a single parent of a child with autism. Whether you coordinate the details of your estate plan with your child's other parent or not, a plan should be made to guarantee that you have organized things the way you want them for your child.

What about a Will?

In short, a will is a legal document. Its purpose is to carry out the distribution of your assets (property and the like) and to specify who will care for your minor child according to your wishes. You may have created a will when you got married, established a legal union with your partner, and/or had a baby. And, most likely, you and your ex made special arrangements in your will

regarding your child with autism. However, now that you are a single parent, it's time to update and/or create a brand new will that will reflect your current situation to address the special needs of your child with autism.

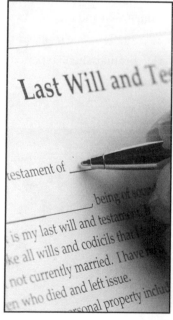

NOTE: You may need to consult with a lawyer who understands—or at least has some knowledge of—autism.

A Tragedy Can Become a Catastrophe: Karen's Story

Karen, a 46-year-old schoolteacher, received a diagnosis of lupus when she was in her early 30s. Her health had been up and down for years, which only made it more difficult for her to care for her 9-year-old daughter, Megan, who received a diagnosis of autism when she was a toddler. Bob, Karen's husband, was an insurance broker who managed large corporate accounts and spent weeks at a time on the road, traveling away from Karen and Megan. As a result, Karen had to pick up the slack on the home front. Carpooling, therapy appointments, IEP meetings, holidays, birthdays: You name it, and Bob missed it.

After years of trying to hold down the fort alone, Karen realized that she couldn't take it any longer and filed for divorce from Bob. Although they remained friendly during the divorce proceedings, this was a particularly painful decision for Karen. However, nothing prepared Karen for the devastating news she received shortly after their divorce was finalized. Bob was killed in a car accident, leaving Karen to raise Megan alone. To make matters worse, Bob (and Karen) had no estate plan in place, with no will and no trust. They had been meaning to create a plan whenever Bob "had time" to do it, after their assets were separated.

☀ Develop a Plan of Action: Make a Will

There is no substitute for competent legal advice, and you have much to consider. When creating a will, you will be disposing of your assets and selecting the people who will play a significant role in your child's life. Depending on the laws where you live, you may be selecting an executor, a guardian (or guardians) for your child, a trustee for your child's money, and various powers of attorney in the event that you are incapacitated. You'll want to choose people you trust, and you'll need to talk with them about whether they are willing to accept the responsibilities associated with their roles. You may also want to consider a special-needs trust. For further information on wills and special-needs trusts, consult a special-needs attorney.

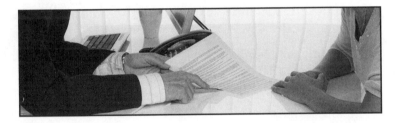

Having a Plan: Marc and Cindy's Story

When Cindy and her husband Marc decided to end their marriage after 18 years, Cindy immediately revised her special-needs trust. She and Marc had three kids together, and their youngest daughter (aged 15) had autism. Cindy wanted to prepare for her kids' futures, especially that of her youngest daughter. She wanted to be sure that her daughters were taken care of after she passed away.

Programs and Plans to Assist Those with Disabilities

Supplemental Security Income, or SSI, is a government program that provides benefits for disabled children and adults in the United States. For more information on SSI, visit *www.socialsecurity.gov.*

Social Security Disability Insurance, or SSDI, is different than SSI. SSDI is a U.S. program that provides benefits for those who have paid Social Security taxes. Certain criteria must be met to be considered for this benefit. For further information on SSDI, visit *www. socialsecurity.gov.*

Building Independence: Jody's Story

Jody received a diagnosis of autism when she was 2 years old. She'd been in special education all throughout school and received a certificate of completion from her high school the week she turned 22. She'd progressed well for the last few years of her program, which focused primarily on preparing her for independence. In fact, Jody's social interactions and ability to work with money (understanding the value of money and making change) improved greatly when she worked 3 days a week at the school's student store.

After she completed high school, Jody's parents sought out an adult day program that would help her continue to improve these skills. Jody's adult day program coordinator helped her look for employment, and eventually Jody was hired to work in a local thrift store. Here, she learned to tag, price, and inventory new items that were brought into the store each week. In addition to the income Jody earned as a part-time employee at the thrift store, her parents helped her apply for monthly Social Security benefits to make ends meet. The income and work experience Jody received contributed to her independence.

CHAPTER 48
Balancing Life as a Single Parent

So many single parents gallantly try to do everything themselves. As a result, they can wind up destroying their health or falling victim to severe depression. As a single parent, finding time for you amidst everyday routines and unexpected challenges at home or at work can be difficult, if not impossible. All your time and attention seems to go straight to the needs of your child with autism. You rarely take any time for yourself, nor do you give your needs any real priority. This is not a healthy perspective (mentally or physically) to have in the long haul, and the earlier single parents realize this, the better their lives will be—for everyone.

It is imperative to come up with healthy solutions. Whether you want to go to an exercise class or merely take a walk, put yourself first and make those things happen. Be creative. For example, if you want to exercise but you don't have child care for your child with ASD, exercise at home while your child exercises with you or watches his favorite show on TV. If you want to take a stroll in the neighborhood and can't leave your child alone, take him with you. You can play games as you walk, or he can listen to his iPod (with earphones) while you enjoy the scenery. When Thomas was little, we took walks regularly. It gave us the opportunity to chat and be silly. One of our favorite walking games was called "Top This." I'd start by stating an outlandish fact, and he'd have to say if he thought it was true or not (like, "Houseflies have eyelashes"). Then, he'd have to top it with an outrageous fact of his own. (Thomas's facts were always much more interesting.) It was a fun way to connect while we walked.

Parents of special-needs children need not give up their lives or things they enjoy simply because they are newly single. They just need to be creative in making those things happen.

Taking Care of You

Self-preservation is said to be the first law of nature. And, although I'd give my right arm to my son if he needed it, I realized pretty early on that if I was going to be an effective single parent, I too needed nurturing—and so do you.

It's not just about finding time for yourself. It's about changing the way you view your situation and shifting your priorities. For me, it was about making sacrifices. I cooked less, cleaned less, and lived on less income. I gave up the need to be "perfect" and for things to be perfect. I made myself a priority and allowed myself to be vulnerable. I even asked for help from family and friends when I needed it.

This was definitely uncomfortable for me, especially at first. In time, I realized that asking for help was not a sign of weakness—it was a sign of a good mother—one who wants to be here for her child not just this month or this year, but for years to come. No one was going to step in and take care of me. So, I decided that I would make myself take "respite time." I did this for 3 hours each week for years. I gave myself permission to take care of myself. Whether I met a friend for coffee, took a nap, or read a gossip magazine, it was my time—and I took it.

And I recommend that you do, too! It takes enormous strength and courage to do what we do, day in and day out. Allow yourself some rejuvenation time to regroup and relax. You'll be a better parent for it. I can't stress this point enough: *To this day, I take time for myself each and every day.* And you can, too.

Survival Tips for Everyday Living

1. *Invest in a house cleaner*
   Give yourself a break and pay someone else to do the cleaning—even if it's only once a month or for the "big" cleaning jobs.

2. *Exercise during lunch*

   Exercise is good for the mind, body, and soul. If you feel like you need a break from the hustle and bustle of work, home, or the kids, get outdoors, take a walk, and breathe the fresh air. Rejuvenate your whole body.

3. *Eat healthy snacks throughout the day*

   Take a few minutes for yourself everyday to EAT! Eating small, healthy snacks throughout the day helps to reenergize the body and keep you sane. Remember to look out for you!

4. *Be social and invite a friend over for a meal*

   Many parents find cooking relaxing. If you need a break but can't seem to get away, invite someone over for a home-cooked meal. You deserve some adult time, too! It's always fun to unwind at home while you "dish and dine" with a friend.

5. *Take a bubble bath with candles*

   There's no better way to relax than to soak in a tub full of bubbles, surrounded by candles. Wash away your troubles and sink into serenity … even if it's only for 20 minutes!

6. ***Get some real rest***
   Recharge your batteries with some extra zzzz's! Whether it's early to bed or late to rise, get the extra sleep you need to revitalize yourself. Rest is important, and so are you.

7. ***Steal a few quiet minutes for yourself***
   Read the Sunday paper over a cup of coffee before the kids get up and start their day, and catch up on some YOU time. You need your special alone time, so take it!

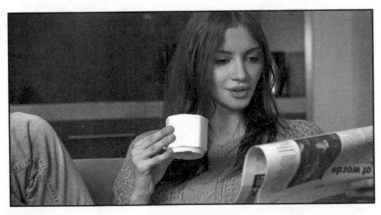

Parents Are People Too

Your new mantra is, *Parents are people, too!* That means YOU. And now that you're flying solo, it's more important than ever to recognize that your needs are important, too. Nurture your newfound independence, because it's all about you now. For years, you've put everyone else's needs ahead of your own, by either choice or necessity. But the good news is … it's your turn now! So, take out a pen and paper and get ready. This next exercise will help you prioritize your future. When I was newly single, I sat down and created goals for the three main areas in my life. As a single parent raising a child on the autism spectrum, I knew that I needed to be organized and focused. You can too!

The focus of Exercise 5 is to develop new goals for yourself in the three main areas of your new life:

- Personal
- Professional
- Financial

Think about this new beginning as an opportunity for you to start over—a fresh start, where you are in charge of you. The best way to help you recreate a new you is by establishing new goals. What have you always aspired to do? If you could spend your time doing anything you wanted, what would you choose to do? Whether your plan was to finish college, take up painting, or sell real estate, redesign your future by mapping how you plan to achieve your new goals. Under each of the three main areas listed previously—personal, professional, and financial—list at least three new goals, anticipated timelines to attain your new goals, and any details that show how you plan to reach these goals.

Examples of Personal Goals

Example #1:
I intend to improve my overall health and well-being. Over the next 12 months, I plan to buy more organic foods at the grocery store and eat more balanced meals that include lean protein, fresh vegetables, and raw fruits. I plan to exercise three times per week by walking during my lunch hour and going to yoga class for

an hour on the weekends to improve my overall core strength and endurance.

Example #2:

I intend to create some special "me" time for myself each day so I feel less stressed and calmer when interacting with my children. Starting tomorrow, I will designate 30 minutes each morning before my children wake up to stretch in a peaceful and quiet environment. In addition, every night before I go to sleep, I will mediate for 20 minutes by myself.

Examples of Professional Goals

Example #1:

As a part-time engineer, my goal is to expand my work hours from a part-time position to a full-time position. I intend to approach my employer about how and why increasing my work hours will improve

my overall job productivity. Over the next 3 months, I will also apply for full-time positions with other companies that are hiring experienced engineers. This will help expand my employment opportunities. My overall short-term goal is to increase my earning potential.

Example #2:
I intend to take a basic computer course to update my overall computer skills. Starting next semester, I plan to complete a beginning computer course offered at my local college so I can become more proficient with my computer. My short-term goal is to learn the most current and highly used computer programs so I can eventually return to the workforce as a receptionist in a medical office on a part-time basis.

Examples of Financial Goals

Example #1:
I intend to reduce my overall personal debt. Over the next two years, I will become free from all outstanding credit card debt. To achieve this goal, I plan to not use any credit cards and to make double payments toward

my credit card debts. In addition, I will develop a monthly budget, monitor my spending, and live within my financial means.

Example #2:

I intend to save money for my son's college tuition. Over the next 4 years, I plan to save 15% of my monthly net income in an interest-bearing account. In addition, I plan to save any and all unexpected bonuses, pay increases, and financial gifts or windfalls and put those funds aside for my son's education, as well.

Set Goals for Yourself

What are your top five *personal* goals as a single parent?

1. _____

2. _____

3. _____

4. _____

5. _____

What are your top five *professional* goals as a single parent?

1. _____

2. _____

3. _____

4. _____

5. _____

What are your top five *financial* goals as a single parent?

1. _____

2. _____

3. _____

4. _____

5. _____

Betsy's Story: Going Out with the Gals

Ever since Hannah was a baby, Betsy made sure she took time for herself. Now that Hannah is a teenager and Betsy is a single parent, Betsy is more determined than ever to maintain her "quiet-time getaways." When she was married, Betsy would schedule a mom's weekend away, three times each year, where she and her four best "mom" friends could rent a beach house, watch sappy movies into the wee hours of the morning, and sleep in until noon without a care in the world (all while her husband Pete looked after Hannah). Betsy absolutely required these long weekends away to re-energize herself for Hannah, and her husband Pete agreed. And why wouldn't he? After all, Pete found time to hunt, fish, or camp with a group of his buddies several times a year. Both parents realized they needed a break from their everyday life from time to time. Everybody needs time away from family responsibilities, and Pete and Betsy seized these opportunities whenever possible. In fact, even though Betsy and Pete have since divorced, they have both continued to take their individual "quiet-time getaways." They recognize how vital it was—and is.

Social Events with Coworkers _____

If your busy work schedule or chaotic home schedule just won't allow for you to slip away for days at a time, fear not. Instead, make it a point to catch a ball game, join a poker game, or meet up with some friends after work for a cocktail. The goal is to find the time to step outside of your busy day-to-day existence and do something just for you. It's okay, really. In fact, you'll be surprised at how it will make you feel. I think so many parents believe that to be a good parent they need to be present and on-call for their kids and spouses 24/7. Not so. Look—parents are people, too. And if you keep that in mind, you will remember how wonderful it feels to do something just for you. Think how wonderful it will be to share that feeling with your family. Whether it's hanging out at a sporting event with your buddies after work or taking a gourmet cooking class with your gal pals, being a single parent doesn't mean you can't do those things. Participating in your "individual" life should not stop because you are a single parent of a special-needs child.

Dating

After ending your relationship, the thought of ever entering into another one may be beyond comprehensible. But, believe it or not, someday you may want a companion to share your time with. And *if* or *when* that time comes, embrace it! *You deserve to be happy!*

Taking It Slow: Paula's Story

When Paula split from her husband of 10 years, she thought the rest of her life would be focused on taking care of her son Joshua. But 5 years after her divorce, she met Paul. Paul was a contracting engineer at the power plant where Paula worked as a technical engineer. After getting to know Paul through several work-related team projects, Paula and Paul realized they had many common interests and really enjoyed each other's company. Thus, dating seemed the next natural step.

Although she felt at ease with Paul and enjoyed spending time with him, many months of dating went by before Paula felt comfortable introducing him to Joshua. By then, Paul knew all about Joshua and his Asperger's syndrome, and he was fascinated by Joshua's special interests, especially Joshua's interest in aircraft carriers. When Paul was young, he too was quite taken with aircraft carriers and still had several model carriers collecting dust on a shelf in his office. With several carefully planned outings between Paula, Paul, and Joshua, Joshua gradually grew to accept Paul as a friend of the family.

As time went on, eventually Joshua came to understand the special relationship between Paul and his mother. After a few years of dating, Paul moved into Paula's home with her and Joshua. This was carried out slowly and over time (a few nights a week to start), so Joshua could get comfortable with the change and have time to adjust to their new "family" living arrangements.

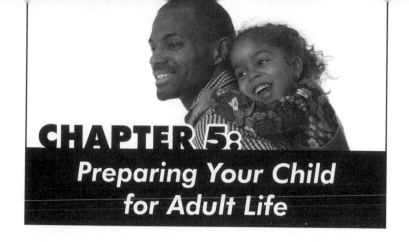

CHAPTER 58
Preparing Your Child for Adult Life

Social Mentoring _____

D oes your child have the skill set to interact socially with friends and/or people in your community? If the answer is "no" or "not quite yet," consider hiring a social mentor for your child to practice these skills.

In the beginning of this book, I started off with a story about how I found my son Thomas asleep at his desk after a long night of studying for his SAT test. I intentionally started the book with that story so you, the reader, could see what can evolve from a single parent's relentless support, together with a child's self-determination and commitment to achieving his future goals. This was not done overnight. My son had a social "life coach" (he referred to her as his "personal assistant") that I hired in the summer months to work with him when he was 15. She was a middle-school teacher in her mid-20s. As Thomas approached adulthood, I believed that he would benefit from spending time with a person of the opposite sex (that is, someone other than his mother).

Because the woman I hired had not worked directly with adolescents on the autism spectrum, and thus had little experience, I provided her with a lot of literature and information about Asperger's syndrome, as well as pertinent information about Thomas—his likes, dislikes, general demeanor, reactions to certain situations, and so on. I also suggested that she spend time with us, just "hanging out," so she could observe firsthand who Thomas was, how he ticked, and how he interacted with other people in the community. As your child grows and matures, so should his opportunities to become socially involved in the community. Learning how to interface with the public and engage with others appropriately is paramount if your child is to become successfully independent.

Building Social Skills

Sometimes a child with ASD can experience anxiety when doing things like meeting a friend at the movies, ordering lunch at a restaurant, or just hanging out at the local bookstore unattended (without you). Help

your child become more comfortable and skilled in these social situations by having her practice these social outings with a social mentor. A newly credentialed teacher, educational aide, or mature peer can make a good social mentor. Since you know your child best, you will instinctively know how to guide your child's mentor to help teach and ultimately improve your child's social skills.

Tips for Social Mentoring

1. *Have your child practice dining out.*
   Let your child interact with the server when ordering her meal at a restaurant. Also, allow her to pay the bill and calculate the tip for the entire meal.

2. *Have your child return an item she purchased from a store.*
   Prior to this exercise, have your child practice the social interaction she anticipates having with the store clerk.

3. *Have your child make dinner reservations for your family.*
   She can do this over the phone, giving the date, time, and number of people in the dinner party.

4. *Have your child ask for driving directions from a stranger.*
   Create a scenario where your child is responsible for getting you both from point A to point B. She will need to determine whom is the most appropriate

person to ask (as well as why he or she is the most appropriate person in that setting). This is *always* a good skill to have.

NOTE: Children on the autism spectrum can be terribly naive and, as a result, their safety can be in jeopardy. When advising your child on how to interface with a stranger, always have him or her direct questions to an employee in a uniform, if possible. If an employee is not available, then suggest having your child ask for help from a mother who is accompanied by children, as this is the type of person that is likely to be most helpful.

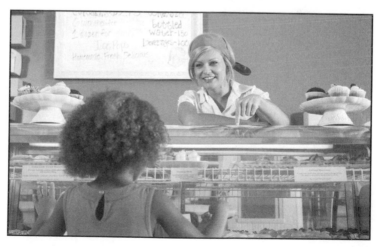

5. *Have your child be responsible for making her next personal appointment.*

   If it's possible to do this in person, have your child make a face-to-face appointment with the receptionist at the dentist, orthodontist, or beauty salon.

A Mentor Can Be a Big Help: Bruce's Story

It was the summer of Bruce's sophomore year of high school when his father Peter decided to hire a mentor for him. Although Bruce was exceptionally bright academically, he was a social recluse. During the school year, he ate lunch alone every day and interacted very little in his classes. On the weekends, he occupied himself by playing video games and watching YouTube videos.

As time went by, Peter became increasingly concerned about Bruce's inability to engage with his peers, and he devised a plan to address the issue. Fortunately, Peter's neighbor had a daughter named Leslie (a freshman in college) who'd just returned home for the summer and was looking for work. Although Bruce and Leslie had never met, Peter hired Leslie to work with Bruce 5 days a week to practice interacting in the community. The goal was for Leslie to work with Bruce on improving some basic community life skills, while building his self-confidence.

Together, Leslie and Bruce decided what "community skills" they would practice each day. Some days they selected a destination and determined what form of public transportation to take to get there. Other days they practiced shopping, cooking, and sharing a meal together. By the end of the summer, Bruce was able to wash his own clothes, balance his own checkbook, and prepare several simple meals, among other things. Not only did Bruce benefit from the community life skills he'd practiced all summer, but he also had the advantage of engaging with Leslie socially on a daily basis. This kind of regular social interaction increased his self-confidence. The experience was invaluable for Bruce.

Leslie says, "Although I'd never done anything like this before, when Peter approached me about Bruce and explained what his difficulties were and how I might help, I felt like I could be of use. I've always been an extremely sociable person, and in working with Bruce, I understood better how being social doesn't come naturally for everyone. The experience also made me aware of other people's differences. For some, communicating is a skill that must be well practiced. That was also the case with Bruce. By the end of the summer, I have to say, Bruce really came out of his shell. I found him to be a sweet kid, with a good sense of humor. I really enjoyed his company, and I would work with him again in a heartbeat."

"Working with Leslie over the summer was weird at first," said Bruce. "I told my dad I just wanted to be alone. I wasn't unhappy or lonely by myself. But, after I got to know Leslie, I did feel more comfortable with her. I found it pretty easy to give my opinion or even disagree with her about something without getting upset. After a while, I actually liked hanging out with her."

Peter felt that Bruce learned a lot from working with Leslie over the summer. "Even though I felt like I took a chance with Leslie, as she had no real experience in working with children on the autism spectrum, she was compassionate and was an extremely patient person," said Peter. "She and Bruce seemed to hit it off right away—a good sign. In the end, not only did Bruce gain numerous community life skills, but he improved his ability to communicate with others more readily. I'm encouraged by his progress and hope it continues."

NOTE: It's often good to have a mentor of the opposite sex work with a teen with ASD, as it provides an opportunity for the teen to better understand and observe gender differences, social behavior, nonverbal communication, and the difference between a friend and a date.

A Little Bit of Direction Goes a Long Way: Sandra's Story

Sandra was 19. She'd graduated from high school with very good grades the year before, but she had not done anything since. She hadn't applied to any colleges, because she couldn't make a decision about which college to attend. She refused to submit applications for any part-time jobs, as she couldn't find one she felt was worthy of her time and talent. She'd always been considered "gifted," with an IQ measuring somewhere in the mid-150s. However, her only interests were the fashion industry and the artistry of makeup. She spent most of her days thumbing through fashion magazines and celebrity Web sites in search of the latest fashion styles and cutting-edge designers.

Camille, Sandra's mother, worked full time as a critical-care nurse. She worked the swing shift, which left little time during the day for her to spend with Sandra. Although Camille admired Sandra's intense interest in the fashion world, she had a difficult time motivating her to look for work so she could gain some experience in anything relating to fashion or makeup. She tried to explain to her daughter that she needed to focus on starting from the ground up. That's how you obtain the most knowledge. Then, she decided to hire a mentor for Sandra—someone who was familiar with fashion, makeup, and retail.

After shopping at Macy's one day, Camille stopped by the makeup counter and approached an employee named Kim. Kim was 22 and had worked for Macy's since her senior year of high school. After talking to her for a while, Camille asked Kim if she'd be interested in working with her daughter Sandra as a mentor. Camille told Kim about Sandra and explained her fascination with fashion and makeup. She also explained that, although Sandra was very bright, she was extremely awkward around people, which hampered her chances for employment in her area of interest—a very social setting. After several more conversations and a face-to-face meeting with Sandra, Kim agreed to work with Sandra two days a week, in addition to working at Macy's.

The goal was for Kim to work with Sandra on improving some fundamental social skills to prepare her for communicating better with people in the community (and potentially in the workplace). Kim and Sandra also worked on improving Sandra's verbal and nonverbal communication skills, self-awareness, personal appearance, and self-confidence. They role-played social scenarios involving customer service and practiced interacting with "pretend" coworkers. Eventually Sandra realized that although she loved fashion, she was not cut out for retail sales or interfacing with customers or fellow employees. Ultimately, Sandra decided to apply for college and major in fashion design.

Kim said, "Working with Sandra was actually a learning experience for me. I discovered a lot about her and how she thought. I learned that because she had her heart set on working in the fashion industry, she was only focused on design and styling and nothing else. Sandra wanted nothing to do with sales. And, as it turned out, because she was very straightforward and often blunt when she spoke, she came across a bit rude—which would not be good in a customer service job. In the end, I think she realized that she didn't enjoy working with people at all. It was not her cup of tea. She prefers to be on her own and seemed glad to sign up for college courses related to fashion instead of working with customers face to face."

Sandra says, "I didn't mind meeting Kim. She seemed nice enough. I know my mom hired Kim to teach me about retail and fashion, since Kim worked at Macy's. The problem

was, when I watched her at work a few times and role-played interacting with customers, I didn't like it. I decided to pursue fashion another way."

Camille originally wanted to help motivate Sandra to pursue her dreams, and, in a way, she did just that. "Since Kim had some experience in retail sales, I thought she could show Sandra what's involved in that field," Camille says. "I had no idea it would be so unpleasant for Sandra. But, because of the experience, I do think that Sandra realized rather quickly that 'sales' is not her forte. As a result, Sandra agreed to register for some fashion classes. Overall, I thought it was a good learning experience for Sandra. She discovered the difference between her *interests* and her *skills*."

Finding a Social Tutor: Scott's Story

Scott was a 27-year-old man with limited social skills. He'd worked for 8 years as a maintenance supervisor at one of the public high schools in town. He lived alone in a rented room near his parents' home, not far from his job. He spent most of his weekends alone, with the exception of Sunday-night dinners with his parents. He was lonely and finally expressed to his parents one night at dinner that he'd like help with developing friendships. His mother, Audrey, put Scott in touch with a gentleman named John, a math tutor she'd known for years from her church. Although Scott was not looking for a math tutor, John was the same age as Scott, and Audrey thought John could offer some pointers to Scott on how to join some local clubs or participate in community events. Scott had been painfully shy his whole life, and that made it difficult for him to develop friendships.

After speaking to Scott on the telephone, John agreed to meet him for coffee. When Scott shared that he wanted to become more connected with the community but didn't know how to go about it, John agreed to help. To start, he invited Scott to a few church functions and helped him learn how to create "small talk" when socializing with others. Over time,

Scott became a regular at church social events. He attended several new social activities in an effort to create opportunities to be around others and, hopefully, develop true friendships.

John says, "Scott seemed like a really nice guy. I think his biggest issue was that he felt so socially awkward in a group. After meeting some of my friends at church, he seemed to become more comfortable at social group outings."

Scott was happy to get together with John from time to time. "His friends seemed nice, and I got the chance to do things I wouldn't ordinarily do, like play games, go to dinner, or see a movie," said Scott. "I'm glad I made the effort to join a group. I'm happier."

Audrey and her husband were thrilled that Scott showed some interest in being with other people. "For most of his childhood, Scott preferred to be by himself, rather than with his peers," said Audrey. "Thank goodness he has found a friend and mentor in John. He really enjoys participating in the adult group activities with our church. We're so pleased for him."

NOTE: Immaturity, social anxiety, and unrealistic expectations can hinder the success of a person with ASD when pursuing goals toward his or her independence.

"Failure to launch," for example, is of great concern for parents of these young adults. Thus, the more opportunities for social interaction, the more experience these folks will have when they interface in the community.

Approaching Adulthood

Believe it or not, your child will grow up and reach adulthood. This is an exciting time in your child's life. As that day approaches, you'll need to prepare him (and yourself) for this very important milestone! By the age of 18, he'll be free to do things without your consent, involvement, or knowledge. For instance, he can apply for a driver's license, register to vote, buy tobacco, drink alcohol legally in some states, and even get married without your knowing!

Educate your adult child with autism so he understands that with these rites of passage comes great responsibility. For example, if your child earns an income, he will most likely be required to pay income tax on that income. If he commits a crime, he will have to face the consequences of the legal system for that crime. If he enters into (agrees to) a contract of some kind, he will be required to honor his agreement. As an adult, many of the decisions he makes will affect his future. And, because every person with autism has varying levels of intellectual and cognitive ability, understanding those decisions (and the concordant responsibilities, possible ramifications, and outcomes) is imperative.

Penny's Story: Realizing It's Time to Let Go

"Does your child need your help, or do you need to help your child?"

This was the question Penny found herself asking over and over again, as her son reached his teens. Penny had been advocating for her son, Ben, since he received a diagnosis of autism back in the first grade. Penny had volunteered in Ben's elementary-school classes, chaperoned his field trips, helped out in the school library, and even signed up for yard duty to protect him from potential bullies at recess.

For years, her life revolved around Ben's needs. To this day, Penny had never missed an IEP meeting to advocate for Ben's lawful Free Appropriate Public Education. Ben, now 17, was entering his junior year of high school and had recently informed Penny that he was capable of doing things on his own. He said he "would no longer require her services." He further informed Penny that he intended to get his learner's permit so he could start driving himself to school, instead of having her do it. Penny was both shocked and proud. She realized that perhaps it was time for her to step back and let go of what had long been her responsibility. She'd been used to doing everything for Ben for so many years, she hadn't realized that her role in Ben's life was changing.

Even with Penny's recent and profound revelation, however, she learned that old habits can be hard to break.

Penny told Ben that he needed to complete a driver's education course online, sign up for a behind-the-wheel class, and prepare for the written driver's permit test at the Department of Motor Vehicles (DMV). To her surprise, Ben announced that he'd already filled out the online course application and just needed her credit card number to pay for the course (as she promised she would). Shortly thereafter, Ben completed the course—and aced it. Penny was flabbergasted. Did her son really coordinate this without her help? Penny was equally surprised by the sequence of events that followed.

She asked Ben if he had his birth certificate and his online driver's education completion form. "You know you'll need to give those two documents to the DMV before you can take your written driver's permit test today, right?" Penny reminded Ben.

"Of course," Ben replied confidently.

Penny and Ben stood together in the long line of people at the DMV. Finally, a man waved Ben up to the window to help him. Penny stood beside Ben, ready to be of service as he turned over his lengthy pile of forms and documents. The man pointed past Penny and said, "Please step back behind that line, Miss."

Confident that he was not referring to her, Penny looked blankly around the room and did not move. "Miss?" the man said again, this time waving his hands as he spoke. Again, Penny briefly glanced around the room. When she finally locked eyes with the man behind the counter, she quickly realized she was the only "Miss" the man was referring to. She sheepishly took several large steps backward and stumbled into a chair, where she quickly sat down (behind the line). Meanwhile, Ben stood at the window and finished filling out his paperwork (by himself). As time ticked by, Penny sat and listened to Ben and the man talk. Although Ben didn't "need" her, at times, Penny found herself wanting to interject, explain, or answer some of the questions Ben was being asked by the man behind the window. But, she didn't! Instead, Penny sat quietly, wiggling her foot back and forth, pretending to busy herself with an old crossword puzzle she found at the bottom of her purse. She reminded herself that she wasn't invited to participate in Ben's conversation. She had been banished from the window, and she bit her tongue. There might as well have been a sign that read, "No hovering parents allowed. Your kids can do this by themselves."

Pretty soon, the man finished reviewing Ben's paperwork. He directed Ben (and only Ben) to yet another long line so he could get his picture taken.

Penny continued to observe Ben from where she sat, and she subtly tried to get his attention. He ignored her. After

Ben had his picture taken, he was given a written test and a pencil and was escorted to another area to take his written test. Penny sat patiently by, waiting and watching the clock. She wondered, "Will he pass his test? What if he doesn't pass? What if …?"

Just then, Ben appeared with his driver's permit and said, "Well, I passed. Let's go." Penny was speechless.

"Does your child need your help, or do you need to help your child?" In the end, Penny realized that her son was maturing, and, in doing so, he needed her less and less. And, *that is a good thing!*

Taking Steps toward Independent Living: Helping Your Child Achieve Independence

The road toward independence is paved with developing skills and abilities. While not all of our children with autism will be ready to live independently at 18 —or later—it is a goal that we should keep our eyes on. The more ways your special-needs child can demonstrate his self-sufficiency, the more independence he will achieve as an adult. Things like self-care, self-advocacy, education, employment, and social adeptness in the community are stepping stones toward achieving independence. Is your child with autism autonomous and able to live independently?

You can help by preparing your adult child to become as socially, emotionally, and financially independent as possible. For some parents, the plan may be helping to prepare their child for college or a vocational program, employment, and, eventually, self-sufficiency. For others, the plan may be preparing their child for part-time work, an internship, or a volunteer position. Yet another option may include helping their child enter into an adult day or residential program (many adult day programs provide job- and life-skills training). Equally important, your child will need to learn (to the best of his ability) how to become included as part of the community.

As a single parent, guiding your child toward reaching his greatest potential may seem exponentially more challenging at times. But, no matter what your situation is, remember that many children on the autism spectrum have tremendous strengths and abilities and aspire to have an independent lifestyle. Try to foster their need for independence and encourage their hopes and dreams. In the end, your child's interests and needs will help you guide him or her toward living a happy, healthy, productive, and independent life (whatever that may be).

Independence Checklist

1. *Self-Care Skills*

   Self-care skills are necessary for children and young adults on the autism spectrum to learn and maintain. First and foremost, teach your child about daily personal hygiene. This is critical! Bathing, wearing clean clothes, and putting together a presentable wardrobe are important when interacting with others in the community. Teach your child the importance of having clean teeth and combed hair. Whether your child is going to work or participating in a program, what she wears and how she looks are important in terms of how she will be received by others.

NOTE: Whether you and your child with ASD are the same gender or not, as a single parent it is important for you to teach your child how to maintain his or her hygiene. For example, for both males and females, it is important to know how and why hair should be washed, combed, and cut, teeth brushed, deodorant applied, legs and underarms shaved for females (and face shaved for males), feminine hygiene products used properly during menstruation for females, and appropriate and clean (and ironed if necessary) clothing worn. Explain why good hygiene is a requirement for your child's overall health, as well as how he or she will be perceived by others in the community. It matters!

2. *Life Skills*

Ask your adult child to practice basic life skills, such as cooking, cleaning, and buying her own groceries (with her own money). Educate her on the importance of managing her money, budgeting,

and paying her household bills correctly and timely. Teaching your child to use public transportation is another important life skill, and one that will foster her independence. The more independent living skills she can learn to practice by herself, the more independent she will become later in life, thereby having to rely less on you.

3. *Self-Advocacy Skills*

   Self-advocacy begins with self-awareness. Educate your adult child with ASD about his diagnosis and how and when to share that information with others. Have him practice articulating this information so he will feel more comfortable when expressing himself and/or when asking for assistance in a work, educational, or community setting. Becoming comfortable with self-advocacy requires preparation and practice. And, with practice comes improved skill.

4. *Secondary Education and Training*

   Whether your child's path leads him to higher education, vocational training, or a workability program, social growth and development are essential. Encourage your adult child to improve his study skills, time-management skills, and task-building skills. To reach independence, your child must understand the value of self-motivation, responsibility, and dependability.

5. *Employment*

Job-search skills, résumé writing, and interviewing skills are essential when seeking employment, internships, or any kind of volunteer work. Understanding subtle body language and nonverbal cues in conversations can be difficult and often eludes children and young adults on the autism spectrum. These fundamental skills and subtle nuances must be learned, as they are especially critical when embarking on new experiences in the workplace. The same is true for understanding the importance of following directives, being a team player, and meeting deadlines.

In Closing ─────────────────

As a single parent, I have learned so many things about myself. Not only have I uncovered the strong, resourceful, and determined woman that I am, but I've also had to embrace many challenging experiences, difficult choices, and complex situations along the way. All of these life lessons have helped prepare me for raising a child on the autism spectrum. I hope you find this book useful for guiding you on your path as a single parent, as well!

Epilogue

After raising my son Thomas for the past 13 years as a single parent, drum roll please …

I remarried! Turns out, I had a "Plan B" and a "Plan C"! After dating for a number of years, I married my longtime significant other. Now, my family of two has grown into a family of five. My wonderful husband Scott and I have three growing boys, ranging from ages 17 to 23.

We considered the blending of our families carefully and thoughtfully before we moved ahead. The timing was especially important and was a critical factor in our decision about when and how to unite our family.

Thomas admires and respects his stepfather and stepbrothers and enjoys spending time with them—and the feeling is mutual. All three boys have very different interests, talents, and skills. This often makes for especially stimulating conversations.

Although there are now five of us, Thomas and I still make it a point to spend time together—just the two of us. Whether it's sneaking off to catch the latest movie or grabbing a bite to eat in town, I try and create regular opportunities for some special one-on-one time, so we can "check in" with one another. It's been a useful way for us to stay connected and keep communication open between us.

Portrait by Linda Johnson, Linda Johnson Photography
www.lindajohnson.com

Frequently Asked Questions

Will my child with autism be worse off for growing up in a single-parent home?

Try and make decisions that best fit your situation as it develops. It's difficult to predict the future of your child and how her life will unfold. It's hard to make assumptions about your child's future and well-being. Focus on living in the moment and being the best parent you can be—and your child will be the better for it.

Will I be able to handle my child's behavioral outbursts alone as a single parent?

It can be scary raising a child alone—especially a child with unpredictable behavior. Resources are available to help guide you or even intervene. Remember that it's okay to ask for help when you need to. It takes a village to raise a family—especially a single-parent family. Utilize the resources in "your village."

How will I make ends meet by living on just one income?

It may be financially difficult at times when you have to rely on only one income. Many parents struggle to pay their bills these days, even those with two incomes. However, it can be done. My advice is to be strategic with your financial plan—develop a plan and set your financial priorities. Create a monthly budget and live by it! Where there's a will, there's a way. Be resourceful. Have confidence in your ability to run a financially sound household!

Are there ASD services that I can get at a reduced rate as a single parent with a limited income?

Sometimes. Depending on your financial circumstances, you may be eligible for a reduced rate, also known as a "sliding scale." Many service providers offer this to their clients on the basis of their income level. Also, if finances are tight, you can always inform your ASD service providers about your financial situation and ask for a fee reduction. It never hurts to ask.

I can't imagine ever starting a relationship with someone new after my ugly divorce. Wouldn't it be better to remain single?

You should consider a relationship with someone when and if you're ready. Only you will know when or if the time is right! Don't let your recent circumstances dictate your future. Live in the moment, not your past. If you meet someone down the road, consider it then. You don't have to decide the rest of your life today.

How will a new relationship with someone who already has children affect my child with special needs?

It's difficult to predict. Change is often challenging for any child, let alone a child with special needs. It's good to take your time when starting a new relationship with someone who has children of his or her own. It's smart to be observant, cautious, and sensitive with regard to family dynamics. Bringing together families requires an adjustment period. Most importantly, ask yourself how the decision may affect your own child, now and in the future.

What will happen to my special-needs child if something happens to me?

No one knows for sure what the future holds. But, to ease your anxiety about what will happen to your child after you're gone, it would be good to put a plan in place now. Many single parents have drawn up a will and/or trust to ensure that they have their desires, wishes, and requests in writing, in the best interests of their child. Looking into these options may alleviate some anxiety, while helping to prepare you and your child for a future without you.

Should I tell my child's special-education teacher about my family situation?

When your family situation changes, your child will be affected, as well. She may express herself on how she's feeling about her new family situation in an emotional and/or behavioral way at school. Inform your child's teacher about your new family circumstances, so your child's teachers and others can be understanding and supportive of her.

How can I apply for financial assistance to help raise my teen with autism, now that I'm a single parent with less income?

Depending on your financial needs, oftentimes federal, state, and/or local agencies provide assistance to single-parent families who have special-needs children. Research what the options are in your specific area by contacting all three government levels. Your child or teen may qualify for support on the basis of her diagnosis and/or special needs according to the law.

Should I hire a mentor for my teenage son with Asperger's syndrome? He's not particularly social.

Parenting a teenager alone can be difficult, regardless of your circumstances. If you find that your teenager needs some assistance developing his social skills and/or life skills, hiring a mentor could be very useful. Someone who is skilled and knowledgeable in the areas in which your teenager requires help could greatly improve your teen's ability to interact socially, as well as his independent living skills. Look into hiring college students (for example, those majoring in psychology or child development), camp counselors (perhaps those who have experience with special-needs kids), or peer mentors (maybe an Eagle Scout or a swim coach). All are viable options.

My daughter has tactile issues with food. How can I get my daughter to eat better?

It's not easy for anyone to change her dietary preferences. If your child has a restricted diet because she has tactile issues, texture aversions, or a limited interest in food, encouraging her to expand her food repertoire can be tricky. My advice is to start slowly, by introducing one new food item at a time. If your child struggles with "new" things, overwhelming her with too many choices can backfire. Allow her to start with one new item (a small bite) in her mouth with the option of spitting it out or swallowing it. If she has control of how she introduces new foods into her diet, it will alleviate the anxiety of having to eat them (eventually).

My son with autism has made so much progress lately. Will he regress if my husband and I change our living situation?

That's hard to say. Your child may or may not regress, for a number of different reasons. Rather than worry about what "might" happen, focus on making the transition to a different living situation go smoothly for your child. The calmer you can make the environment, the smoother the transition is likely to be. If you fear that your child may regress, you may want to enlist the help of a psychologist to assist in the process. Take one day at a time. Things improve over time, not overnight.

My preteen daughter has been acting out at school ever since her mother and I separated. What's the best way to handle that?

If you feel that there is a direct correlation between your daughter's behaviors and your new family situation, you should immediately include your child's other parent and discuss the issue with those involved at her school. At some point, whenever it's appropriate, include your daughter in the conversation about her behavior and discuss possible solutions. At the end of the day, your child needs to feel secure and supported by both parents.

My special-needs son just graduated from high school with a diploma. I'm not sure if he should apply for college or get a job?

Every child develops at a different rate. This is especially true for those with a disability. Find out where your child excels naturally (along with his areas of interest) and guide him in the direction that would provide him with the most success. If he is great academically and wishes to pursue that route, encourage him to continue with higher education. If school is not his thing, but working or volunteering is, then encourage him to pursue that route. Help him to find his niche. Have him take an aptitude test so he can discover where he excels. Consider hiring a job coach to help prepare him for employment. Helping him find his way is how you can be most useful as a parent.

My daughter is having trouble with her studies in college. Although she has an autism diagnosis, she refuses to disclose that information to her college instructors. What can I do to help her?

Self-advocacy can be advantageous for young adults who recognize and accept that they have a disability and require assistance in college. Only your child can decide if and when she wants to advocate for herself. And, if she does, disclosing personal information about herself can be a difficult and emotional decision. You can explain to your daughter the pros and cons of disclosing her personal information, but it's up to her if she chooses to do so. Role-playing with your child about how and when to disclose her personal information and how it relates to her disability can be extremely useful.

My ex and I split up over a year ago. Ever since then, my 7-year-old son has become more and more withdrawn. What can I do?

Change can be hard for anyone—particularly for those on the spectrum. If your child withdraws emotionally, give him some time to adapt to his new situation. If you feel that his behavior is not improving over time and he seems to engage less with you and others, pursue professional help from a trained psychologist. A professional can be helpful when dealing with a child who is struggling with a divided family.

My teenage son with high-functioning autism is extremely argumentative at times. It started shortly after his father and I ended our 20-year marriage. What can I do to stop this behavior?

Recognize that your son has just experienced a major change in his life. Allow him some time to react. If his behavior continues, explain to him that although you understand how he might be feeling, his argumentative behavior is not appropriate. Discuss with him some alternatives and talk about more appropriate ways to express his feelings. Also, you might investigate family counseling or individual therapy. Ask a professional to help you teach your son about ways to interact with you effectively.

Even though I've been unhappy for years, I feel so guilty for ending my marriage. How do I move past these feelings of guilt?

It's natural to have a number of feelings—including guilt—when going through such a huge life transition. Chances are that your decision has created multiple changes that are affecting you and your family. As a result, you may be having mixed emotions about your decision. That's okay. Allow yourself time to grieve the loss of your marriage. It's totally normal. Focus on the life you see for yourself in the future. You and your ex deserve to be happy.

When my wife told me she wanted to separate, I was shocked. I can't imagine being a single parent and raising my twin boys with autism on my own. How will I manage?

It's hard when you come to the realization that your life is not what you thought it was going to be. If you're having a difficult time accepting the reality of your circumstances, perhaps it would be good to seek out professional therapy to help you understand your situation and deal with it in the most productive way. Everyone going through a difficult time deserves the emotional support he or she needs.

I feel so overwhelmed sometimes. Even though my husband has partial custody, I'm the primary parent in charge of my son with Asperger's syndrome. What can I do to have less stress?

Take the time to de-stress. For example, whenever you don't have your son, start doing things that you enjoy and that you find relaxing. It can be hard to be a single parent, so make it a priority to take care of yourself. You have to be well to feel well. Whether it's going for a walk, taking a bubble bath, or getting coffee with a friend, do something that will relax your mind, body, and spirit so you feel less overwhelmed. You need to take care of you!

I'm so used to having my daughter around me 100% of the time. Now that my ex has her half of the time, I feel so lonely without her.

Change is difficult for everyone, including parents. A lot of emphasis is placed on how the child will adjust when a family divides, but the truth is, it affects parents, too. It's natural to feel lonely sometimes, because your time is spent differently now. Take that time and do something solely for you. It's your special time. Enjoy yourself.

I'm a stay-at-home parent. Because of this big transition (divorce) in our lives, I'm nervous about how returning to work will affect my child.

Transition is hard. And, children on the autism spectrum typically have a difficult time with transition (of any kind). But, if you need to return to the workplace before or after your child is in school, then that's what you need to do. However, if you are in a position (financially) to wait, and you feel that both you and your child would benefit from you being at home during this transitional period, by all means, take your time before returning to work. Nurture your child and yourself through this process.

How will I be able to afford my child's speech therapy on my own?

You may not be able to afford it. You may need to temporarily alter your child's speech therapy services (or other therapeutic services) until you get back on your feet financially. Remember: Basic necessities come first. If necessary, it's okay to stop one or two of your child's therapeutic services temporarily. A healthy meal, a safe home, and a loving parent are most important.

My son is 21 years old—a legal adult. Although he lives with me, and I adore him, I'm single and ready to share my life with someone. How do I get my son to understand he needs to be independent and live on his own?

I understand perfectly. Hopefully your adult son with special needs has honed his life skills to where he's at least self-sufficient. Does he have the ability to grocery shop, cook, clean, and manage his finances? Can he take public transportation (or drive a car) safely? Can he manage his banking, monthly budget, and personal hygiene and make medical and dental appointments independently? Can he support himself financially? Does he participate in any community events? Does he require any assistance with independent living skills or social and life-skills training? These are questions you may want to consider to ensure that your adult special-needs child is ready to live independently.

Resources

As a single parent, it's always good to build a resource library to assist you in furthering your knowledge on autism-related topics. This chapter includes a collection of relevant autism resource Web sites, book suggestions, and magazine Web sites specific to autism. These can help you build your knowledge base in areas that are relevant to your own unique circumstances.

Autism-Related Web Sites

www.aspergersresource.org
> A general resource site for parents with a child or young adult with an autism spectrum disorder.

aspergersyndrome.org
> An online information and support center for Asperger's syndrome.

www.aspennj.org
> A site that provides families and individuals with education, support, and advocacy for those affected by ASD.

www.tonyattwood.com.au
> A site to guide parents, professionals, and people with Asperger's syndrome and their partners.

www.usautism.org
> Provides information about education, training, and other accessible resources to those with autism in partnership with local and national projects.

www.orionacademy.org
> A quality college preparatory program for secondary students, whose academic success is compromised by a neurocognitive disability such as Asperger's syndrome.

autismcollege.com
> An educational resource for parents, families, and professionals in the autism community.

autismnow.org/on-the-job/employment-research-and-reports
Information regarding employment options for people with ASD.

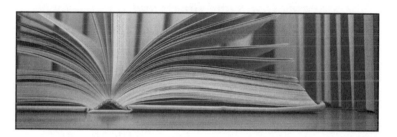

ASD Books

■ General Books for Kids

Too Smart for Bullies
by Robert Kahn and Sharon Chandler

Ellie Bean the Drama Queen! How Ellie Learned to Keep Calm and Not Overreact
by Jennie Harding

The Child with Autism Goes to Town: The Go Anywhere Guide—250 Tips for Community Outings
by Kathy Labosh

Understanding Death and Illness and What They Teach about Life: An Interactive Guide for Individuals with Autism or Asperger's and Their Loved Ones
by Catherine Faherty and Gary B. Mesibov

Taking Care of Myself: A Hygiene, Puberty, and Personal Curriculum for Young People with Autism
by Mary Wrobel

My Friend with Autism: A Coloring Book for Peers and Siblings
by Beverly Bishop

Overcoming Loss: Activities and Stories to Help Transform Children's Grief and Loss
by Julia Sorensen

■ General Books for Teens and Young Adults

Asperger's and Girls
> by Tony Attwood, Temple Grandin, Teresa Bolick, Catherine Faherty, Lisa Iland, Jennifer McIlwee Myers, Ruth Snyder, Sheila Wagner, and Mary Wrobel

Middle School: The Stuff Nobody Tells You About
> by Haley Moss

Life after High School: A Guide for Students with Disabilities and Their Families
> by Susan Yellin

Safety Skills for Asperger Women: How to Save a Perfectly Good Female Life
> by Liane Holliday Willey

■ *Relationship and Sexuality Books*

Intimate Relationships and Sexual Health: A Curriculum for Teaching Adolescents/Adults with High-Functioning Autism Spectrum Disorders and Other Social Challenges
   by Catherine Davies and Melissa Dubie

Autism-Asperger's and Sexuality: Puberty and Beyond
   by Jerry Newport, Mary Newport, and Teresa Bolick

Asperger's Syndrome and Sexuality: From Adolescence through Adulthood
   by Isabelle Hénault

■ *Self-Advocacy Books*

Ask and Tell: Self-Advocacy and Disclosure for People on the Autism Spectrum
   by Ruth Elaine Joyner Hane, Kassiane Sibley, Stephen M. Shore, and Roger N. Meyer

The Integrated Self-Advocacy ISA Curriculum: A Program for Emerging Self-Advocates with Autism Spectrum and Other Conditions
by Valerie Paradiz

■ Transition and Life-Skills Books

Guiding Your Teenager with Special Needs through the Transition from School to Adult Life: Tools for Parents
by Mary Korpi

Transition or Transformation? Helping Young People with Autistic Spectrum Disorder Set Out on a Hopeful Road towards Their Adult Lives
by John Clements, Julia Hardy, and Stephanie Lord

The Social and Life Skills Menu: A Skill Building Workbook for Adolescents with Autism Spectrum Disorders
by Karra M. Barber

Preparing for Life: The Complete Guide for Transitioning to Adulthood for Those with Autism and Asperger's Syndrome
    by Jed Baker

Social Skills for Teenagers and Adults with Asperger Syndrome: A Practical Guide to Day-to-Day Life
    by Nancy J. Patrick

Providing Practical Support for People with Autism Spectrum Disorder: Supported Living in the Community
    by Denise Edwards

Asperger's Syndrome and Adolescence: Helping Pre-teens and Teens Get Ready for the Real World
    by Teresa Bolick

■ *Books on College*

The Parent's Guide to College for Students on the Autism Spectrum
> by Jane Thierfeld Brown, Lorraine Wolf, Lisa King, and G. Ruth Bork

Succeeding in College with Asperger Syndrome: A Student Guide
> by John Harpur, Maria Lawlor, and Michael Fitzgerald

Realizing the College Dream with Autism or Asperger Syndrome: A Parent's Guide to Student Success
> by Ann Palmer

■ *General Books for Parents*

Asperger's Syndrome: A Guide for Parents and Professionals
> by Tony Attwood

Supporting Women after Domestic Violence: Loss, Trauma and Recovery
by Hilary Abrahams

Special Diets for Special Kids: Volumes 1 and 2 Combined—Research and Recipes
by Lisa Lewis

The Parents' Guide to Teaching Kids with Asperger Syndrome and Similar ASDs Real-Life Skills for Independence
by Patricia Romanoski

■ **Books on Careers and Employment**

Developing Talents: Careers for Individuals with Asperger Syndrome and High-Functioning Autism
by Temple Grandin, Kate Duffy, and Tony Attwood

Employment for Individuals with Asperger Syndrome or Non-Verbal Learning Disability: Stories and Strategies
by Yvona Fast

How to Find Work That Works for People with Asperger Syndrome: The Ultimate Guide for Getting People with Asperger Syndrome into the Workplace (and Keeping Them There!)
by Gail Hawkins

Business for Aspies: 42 Best Practices for Using Asperger Syndrome Traits at Work
by Ashley Stanford

DVDs

Asperger Syndrome and Employment: A Personal Guide to Succeeding at Work
by Nick Dubin

Autism and Asperger's Syndrome DVD: An Insightful Presentation
   by Dr Temple Grandin

Exploring Feelings DVD: Cognitive Behaviour Therapy to Manage Anxiety, Sadness and Anger
   by Tony Attwood

Homeschooling the Child with Asperger Syndrome: Real Help for Parents Anywhere and on any Budget
   by Lise Pyles

A Treasure Chest of Behavioral Strategies for Individuals with Autism
   by Beth Fouse and Maria Wheeler

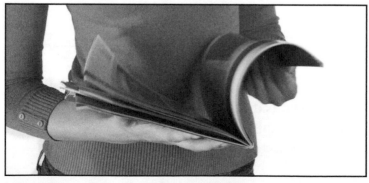

ASD Magazines

Autism-Asperger's Digest
 www.autismdigest.com

Autism Spectrum Quarterly
 www.asquarterly.com

Spectrum Magazine
 www.spectrumpublications.com

The Autism File
 www.autismfile.com

Positively Autism
 www.positivelyautism.com

Parenting Special Needs
 www.parentingspecialneeds.org

Exceptional Parent
 eparent.com

About the Author

Karra Barber-Wada is a full-time mother and advocate for her son, who was diagnosed with Asperger's syndrome at the age of 6. She is the founder and facilitator of a well-established support group for parents of teens and young adults on the autism spectrum. She is the author of *Living Your Best Life with Asperger's Syndrome* and *The Social and Life Skills Menu*. She is a regular contributor to many autism magazines. Karra resides in northern California with her husband and three children.

If you enjoyed this book, you may also like

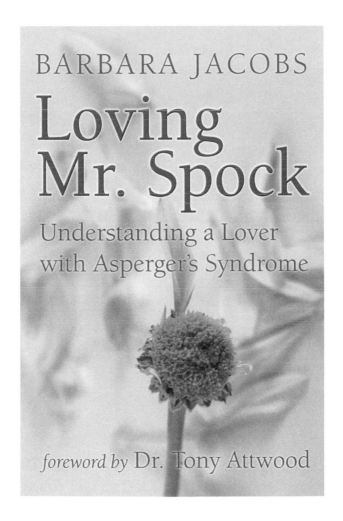

BARBARA JACOBS

Loving
Mr. Spock

Understanding a Lover
with Asperger's Syndrome

foreword by Dr. Tony Attwood

Future Horizons is proud to also publish these titles by Dr Temple Grandin

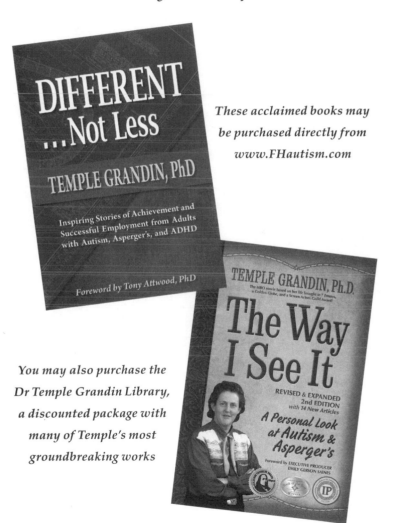

These acclaimed books may be purchased directly from www.FHautism.com

You may also purchase the Dr Temple Grandin Library, a discounted package with many of Temple's most groundbreaking works